Foreword

In an era where companies are not only judged on their profits, but also on the impact they make on the world, commitment to ESG (Environmental, Social, and Governance) principles has become more than an option: it has become an imperative. This book, "ESG: Audit Checklist," is a meticulous guide for those who are looking to venture into the essence of corporate responsibility, aiming for excellence in this new business paradigm.

The concept of ESG has evolved over the years from mere buzzwords to essential pillars of good corporate governance. Stakeholders, whether they are investors, consumers, or communities, are now demanding transparency and accountability from companies in their practices. This demand, combined with the growing awareness of environmental and social risks, has put ESG auditing in the spotlight.

As readers flip through the pages of this book, they will be guided through a journey that begins with an understanding of the fundamentals of ESG and culminates in a comprehensive, functional audit designed to lead any company to excellence in these vital criteria. Each chapter has been structured in such a way as to provide not only information, but also practical tools – in the form of checklist forms – that will ensure that no stone is left unturned.

However, the true essence of this work lies not only in the functionality of its structure, but in the promise of a better future. A promise of more conscious companies, fairer societies and a healthier planet.

If you are looking for a transformation in your organization, so that it not only understands, but also internalizes and acts on ESG principles, this book will be your compass. Through a clear and structured path, we ensure not only the understanding, but also the effective implementation of ESG criteria, elevating your company to levels never reached before.

Get ready to embark on a journey that will not only shape the future of your organization, but also the future of our precious planet. Happy reading and happy transforming!

ESG:

CheckList Auditoria

Fabricio Sales

All rights of this edition are reserved exclusively to the author:
Fabricio Sales Silva
Tel: 55 (12) 997951194
Email: fabricio_salles@yahoo.com.br

Summary

Chapter 1: Laying the Groundwork 15

1.1 – Understanding ESG 15
1.2 – Audit Scope 17
1.3 - The global relevance of ESG for business 19
1.4 - Selection and Categorization of Suppliers 21
1.5 - Implementation of ESG criteria in corporate strategy 23
1.6 - Initial ESG Risk Assessment 25
1.7 - Initial Challenges and Opportunities in ESG 28

Chapter 2: Environmental Assessment . 30

2.1 - Greenhouse Gas (GHG) Emissions 30
2.2 - Energy Efficiency and Renewable Sources 32
2.3 - Water and Waste Management 34
2.4 - Impact on Biodiversity and Ecosystems 36
2.5 - Evaluation of Pollutants and By-Products 38
2.6 - Environmental Impact Mitigation Strategies 40

2.7 - Environmental Commitments and Targets 42

2.8 - Carbon Bonding 44

Chapter 3: Social Approach 47

3.1 - Corporate Culture Assessment 47

3.2 - Health, Safety and Well-being of Employees 49

3.3 - Human Rights 51

3.4 - Engagement with Local Communities 53

3.5 - Diversity and Inclusion 55

3.6 - Training, Education and Professional Development 57

3.7 - Management of Complaints and Feedbacks in the Social part 59

Chapter 4: Corporate Governance 62

4.1 - Organizational Structure and Governance Responsibilities 62

4.2 - Business Ethics and Integrity 64

4.3 - Decision Making Mechanisms 66

4.4 - Transparency and disclosure of information 68

4.5 - Management of Conflicts of Interest 70

4.6 - Rules and Definition of Compliance 72

4.7 - Evaluation and Review of Internal Policies 74

4.8 - Governance Training and Awareness 76

Chapter 5: Supplier Evaluation 79

5.1 - ESG Selection and Qualification of Suppliers 79

5.2 - Supply chain management with a focus on ESG. 81

5.3 - Continuous Monitoring and Evaluation of Suppliers 83

5.4 - ESG Training and Capacity Building of Suppliers 86

5.5 - Ethical Sourcing Policies 88

5.6 - Supplier engagement and feedback 90

5.7 - Compliance rules in the relationship with suppliers 92

5.8 - Supplier Action Plans and Continuous Improvement 95

Chapter 6: Financial Assessment and ESG 97

6.1 - Integration of ESG Risks in Financial Analysis ... 97

6.2 - The Financial Value of Responsible Investment 100

6.3 - Return on Investment (ROI) in ESG Initiatives 102

6.4 - ESG metrics and KPIs in financial performance 104

6.5 - Sustainable Finance Strategies 106

6.6 - Financial Costs associated with ESG implementation 108

6.7 – Financial Market Opportunities and ESG Growth 111

Chapter 7: Engagement and Communication 113

7.1 - ESG Communication Strategies........................... 113

7.2 - Management of Stakeholder Expectations 115

7.3 - Stakeholder Mapping and Prioritization 118

7.4 - ESG communication and reporting tools 120

7.5 - Feedback and Open Dialogue with Stakeholders 122

7.6 - Challenges in ESG communication 124

7.7 - Communication Improvement Strategies 127

7.8 - Community Engagement 129

Chapter 8: Innovation and ESG 131

8.1 - Integration of ESG into the Innovation Strategy 131
8.2 - Sustainable innovations in products and services 133
8.3 - Product Life Cycle Assessment 135
8.4 - Circular Economy Initiatives 137
8.5 - Partnerships and Collaborations for ESG Innovation 139
8.6 - Challenges and opportunities in sustainable innovation 141
8.7 - Goals and Results in ESG Innovations 143

Chapter 9: Monitoring and Continuous Review 146

9.1 - ESG Monitoring Tools and Techniques 146
9.2 - The Importance of Review and Continuous Improvement 148
9.3 - Benchmarking and Peer Comparison 150
9.4 - Organizational Feedback and Learning 152
9.5 - Carbon Footprint Monitoring 154

9.6 - ESG Performance Assessment 156

9.7 - Identification and treatment of non-conformities 158

9.8 - Planning of Corrective Actions 160

Chapter 10: Conclusion and Future Vision 163

10.1 - Future Commitments and Strategic Planning .. 163

10.2 - The evolution of ESG concepts and emerging trends 165

10.3 - The role of corporations in the sustainable future 168

10.3 - The role of corporations in the sustainable future 170

10.4 - Future ESG Audits 172

10.5 - ESG Learning 174

10.6 - Closure and Documentation of the ESG Audit 177

10.7 - Plans to Obtain Green Certificates 179

ESG: CheckList Auditoria 181

Chapter 1: Laying the Groundwork

1.1 – Understanding ESG

In a world of transformations, the understanding and application of ESG (Environmental, Social and Governance) principles have become fundamental for companies and organizations that seek to align with the current and future demands of their stakeholders.

1. What is your organization's official definition of ESG?

2. How are ESG principles integrated into your company's vision and mission?

3. What are the main benefits perceived by the organization by adopting ESG practices?

4. How are employees informed and trained about the importance of ESG and its practical implications?

5. What are the main challenges faced by your organization in implementing and maintaining ESG practices?

6. How does your organization measure the success of its ESG initiatives?

7. Which stakeholders are considered in the formulation and execution of ESG strategies?

8. Is there a responsible person or team dedicated exclusively to the management and supervision of ESG practices?

9. How does the organization ensure that its ESG practices and policies are continuously updated in light of new developments and discoveries in the field?

10. How does the organization communicate its ESG commitments and achievements to its internal and external stakeholders?

In modern times, where the speed of change is the only constant, having a solid understanding of ESG and its effective implementation is more than a simple trend: it is a necessity. It's not just about staying ahead of the competition, it's about ensuring an organization's long-term sustainability, accountability, and integrity.

Each item on this checklist is an invitation for organizations to take a deep dive into their practices and values, ensuring that the essence of ESG is truly embedded in their DNA. The goal is not only to understand ESG, but to experience it in every decision and action.

The current global scenario demands a critical vision and a modern approach to ESG integration. Through this checklist, we hope that organizations can evaluate and realign their strategies, ensuring that their actions truly reflect their commitments. By adopting robust ESG practices, organizations not only solidify their position in the global marketplace but also play a crucial role in building a more sustainable and equitable future for all.

1.2 – Audit Scope

In a world of transformations, the role of ESG (Environmental, Social and Governance) has gained prominence in business and government practices. Integrating these concepts into an organization's routine requires a thorough understanding of the scope of an ESG-focused audit.

1. What is the primary purpose of auditing in relation to ESG principles?

2. Which departments or units of the organization will be included in this audit scope?

3. Are there any specific areas or processes that will be the primary focus of the ESG audit?

4. Does the scope of the audit cover both the organization's internal operations and its relationships with external parties?

5. What are the specific ESG criteria that the audit proposes to assess?

6. Will the audit consider historical practices or will it focus only on the organization's current practices?

7. What will be the key performance indicators (KPIs) used to measure compliance with ESG standards?

8. Does the scope consider all geographic jurisdictions in which the organization operates?

9. Are there any specific time considerations for the audit, such as a specific time window?

10. What resources (human, technological, financial) are required to perform the audit as defined in this scope?

Clearly defining the scope of an ESG audit is key to ensuring that the review is both thorough and relevant. Additionally, it allows the organization to prepare appropriately, ensuring that the necessary resources are available and that stakeholders are informed and engaged in the process.

By finalizing a well-defined audit, organizations have a clearer picture of their strengths and areas for improvement when it comes to ESG. This process not only helps companies improve their practices, but also reaffirms their commitment to sustainable and responsible development. This commitment, coupled with transparent and well-informed action, is crucial to building stakeholder trust and ensuring a resilient position in the global marketplace. Therefore, each item on this checklist is crucial for organizations of all types and sizes to define and fulfill their purpose in the ESG scenario, leading with integrity, innovation, and responsibility.

1.3 - The global relevance of ESG for business

In a scenario marked by constant change, the integration of ESG (Environmental, Social and Governance) principles into business practices has become imperative. The growing global awareness of sustainability and corporate responsibility issues requires organizations to not only understand the relevance of ESG but also adopt these practices into their business models.

1. Does the organization recognize global trends regarding ESG practices?

2. Are there well-defined strategies in place to align business operations with globally accepted ESG standards?

3. Does the company regularly assess its ESG performance against global standards?

4. Is the organization aware of international regulations and laws related to ESG in all markets in which it operates?

5. Are there mechanisms in place to identify and respond to global stakeholders' expectations regarding the organization's ESG performance?

6. Are employees and business partners trained and informed about the global importance of ESG and its impact on business operations?

7. Does the company actively seek global collaborations or partnerships to enhance its ESG practices?

8. Do annual reports and corporate communications reflect the organization's commitment to global ESG relevance?

9. Does the organization have a strategy to manage risks associated with ESG in a global context?

10. Are there any established metrics and indicators to assess the success of integrating ESG practices into the global business context?

Integrating ESG principles into the fabric of business is not just a matter of complying with regulations or achieving certifications. It's about recognizing that business success and resilience in today's global landscape are intrinsically linked to an organization's ability to operate sustainably, fairly, and transparently. In today's business world, the ESG approach is no longer an option but an imperative.

In this context, this checklist serves as an essential tool for organizations to constantly assess and improve their approach to ESG. By following this guideline, companies not only strengthen their position in the global market but also make a positive contribution to a sustainable and equitable future. The path towards full ESG integration requires commitment, vision, and action. With the right tools, organizations can confidently navigate this direction, ensuring lasting benefits for themselves, their communities, and the planet as a whole.

1.4 - Selection and Categorization of Suppliers

In times of accelerated change and increasing demands for sustainability, companies' responsibility is not just limited to their internal operations. The choice and categorization of suppliers has become crucial to ensure that ESG (Environmental, Social and Governance) standards are maintained and amplified throughout the entire value chain.

1. Does the organization have clear ESG criteria when choosing new suppliers?

2. Is there a regular assessment of current suppliers based on ESG criteria?

3. Is there a system in place to categorize suppliers according to their ESG performance?

4. Are suppliers incentivized or trained to improve their ESG performance?

5. Does the company take into account the environmental impact of the products or services provided?

6. Are suppliers evaluated based on their labor practices and human rights?

7. Does the company consider transparency and ethics in the governance practices of its suppliers?

8. Is there a mechanism in place to deal with suppliers that do not meet established ESG standards?

9. Are suppliers recognized or rewarded for excellence in ESG practices?

10. Does the organization have an action plan to encourage continuous improvement in ESG among its suppliers?

Integrating ESG criteria into supplier selection and categorization is more than a due diligence measure; It's a recognition that every link in the supply chain plays a vital role in creating a sustainable future. Companies that lead with vision and intent in this area not only protect their reputation and minimize risk, but also foster innovation, increase customer loyalty, and drive positive change across the industry.

This checklist serves as a key tool for companies to align their supply chain with ESG objectives. With the right focus and decisive actions, it is possible to build a network of suppliers who share a common commitment to operating responsibly and sustainably, benefiting the company, society, and the planet. The adoption of these practices highlights the company as a leader in its industry, ready to meet the challenges of the future and create meaningful opportunities for all involved.

1.5 - Implementation of ESG criteria in corporate strategy

In today's ever-evolving landscape, the demands for corporate responsibility have grown exponentially. The adoption and integration of ESG (Environmental, Social and Governance) criteria into corporate strategy are no longer optional, but essential for the long-term sustainability and success of companies. The implementation of these criteria reflects not only the company's commitment to social responsibility, but also its vision of the future and resilience in a world of transformation.

1. Does the company integrate ESG goals into its long-term strategic planning?

2. Are mechanisms in place to regularly monitor and report on progress against ESG objectives?

3. Do corporate leaders demonstrate visible and active commitment to ESG initiatives?

4. Does the organization invest in ESG training and awareness for its employees at all levels?

5. Are ESG criteria considered in investment decisions and resource allocation?

6. Does the company consider ESG impacts in its risk management?

7. Does the organization maintain an open dialogue with stakeholders about its ESG commitments and progress?

8. Are ESG criteria used to evaluate and reward managers' performance?

9. Does the company establish partnerships or collaborations to enhance the impact of its ESG initiatives?

10. Does the organization periodically review and update its ESG strategy to reflect changes in the external environment and stakeholder expectations?

Adopting ESG criteria in corporate strategy ensures that the company is aligned with the growing expectations of its stakeholders, from customers and investors to the wider community. Those who see ESG as a core element of their strategy realize that it goes beyond mere compliance. Such criteria provide opportunities for innovation, brand enhancement, and the establishment of stronger and more trusting relationships with all stakeholders.

The true implementation of ESG criteria is not an isolated act, but an ongoing process. It requires constant commitment, monitoring, and adjustments. But companies that engage in this process find that integrating ESG into their strategy is not only the right thing to do from an ethical standpoint, but also a smart way to do business. These companies are prepared to meet the challenges of tomorrow, establishing themselves as leaders on the global stage, with clear visions for a more sustainable and equitable future.

1.6 - Initial ESG Risk Assessment

In modern times, the growing awareness of global issues puts pressure on companies to adopt a more responsible stance. The ESG (Environmental, Social and Governance) approach has emerged as a vital tool to ensure that companies remain relevant and sustainable in a changing world. A crucial step in effectively integrating ESG principles is the initial risk assessment, allowing companies to identify vulnerabilities and opportunities across the three dimensions of ESG.

1. Does the company have a formalized process for identifying environmental risks in its operations?

2. Are there mechanisms in place to assess social risks, such as human rights issues or impacts on the local community?

3. Does the company consider governance risks, such as regulatory compliance and ethical practices, in its assessment?

4. Does the organization compare its ESG risks to industry benchmarks or internationally recognized standards?

5. Does the initial assessment consider risks across the value chain, including suppliers and partners?

6. Are there tools or software used to quantify and prioritize ESG risks?

7. Does the company seek feedback from external stakeholders, such as NGOs or experts, during the risk assessment?

8. Is the assessment periodically reviewed to incorporate new information or changes in the business environment?

9. Are risk assessment results communicated internally to ensure alignment across departments and teams?

10. Is there a clear action plan based on the results of the assessment to address significant risks and seize opportunities?

The risks associated with ESG are intrinsic to the business environment. Ignoring them can result in financial losses, reputational damage, and missed opportunities. In contrast, companies that conduct comprehensive and systematic initial ESG risk assessments are better positioned to manage those risks, seize opportunities, and ensure a long-term sustainable operation.

By incorporating a robust ESG risk assessment into their operations, companies not only strengthen their resilience but also solidify their reputation with stakeholders. With proper focus, the initial risk assessment is not seen as an obstacle, but rather as a strategic tool. Over time, this approach becomes a key pillar for decision-making, guiding the company through uncertainty and ensuring that it stays ahead of transformations, ready for the future to come.

1.7 - *Initial Challenges and Opportunities in ESG*

Global transformation, both at the corporate and societal levels, pushes organizations to reevaluate their strategies. Specifically, ESG (Environmental, Social, and Governance) concepts are at the forefront of these changes, promoting a more sustainable, ethical, and inclusive business environment. By addressing the initial ESG-related challenges and opportunities, companies not only demonstrate a commitment to a better future but also strategically position themselves to thrive in the current landscape.

1. Has the company identified key environmental challenges associated with its operations and industry?

2. Are there any strategies outlined to address and mitigate these environmental challenges?

3. What environmental opportunities have been recognized, such as energy efficiency or sustainable production?

4. Is the organization aware of the societal challenges it faces, including diversity, inclusion, and employee well-being?

5. What are the opportunities identified to enhance social impact, such as capacity building programs or partnerships with local communities?

6. Is the company aware of governance challenges, such as integrity, ethics, and transparency?

7. Are there opportunities to improve governance through more robust practices and clear policies?

8. Has the organization considered integrating technological innovations to overcome ESG challenges or explore opportunities?

9. Are stakeholders, such as investors and customers, involved in assessing ESG challenges and opportunities?

10. Are there metrics and indicators in place to monitor and evaluate progress against identified challenges and opportunities?

By focusing on early ESG challenges and opportunities, companies can take a proactive approach, anticipating trends and laying a strong foundation for responsible operation. Active involvement in these areas not only responds to rising stakeholder expectations, but also unlocks potential benefits, from improving reputation to identifying new areas of growth.

Considering the dynamic business landscape, it is vital for organizations to maintain an adaptive posture, ready to face challenges and capture opportunities. By taking the time and resources to properly assess these early aspects of ESG, companies not only strengthen their competitive position but also align with a broader vision of success and sustainability. And as the corporate horizon continues to evolve, these ESG assessments and adjustments ensure that organizations are always ready for the next step.

Chapter 2: Environmental Assessment

2.1 - Greenhouse Gas (GHG) Emissions

In a changing world, concern about greenhouse gas (GHG) emissions is at the center of global attention. With an increasing focus on sustainability and environmental responsibility, organizations are being pushed to understand, monitor, and reduce their emissions.

1. Does the company have an up-to-date inventory of all its GHG emission sources?

2. Are there procedures in place to regularly measure and report these emissions?

3. Are the emission data verified and validated by an independent third party?

4. Has the organization set clear targets for emissions reductions within a set timeframe?

5. Are there action plans in place to achieve the reduction targets set?

6. Is the company aware of local and international regulations related to GHG emissions and is it compliant with them?

7. Are both direct GHGs (from the operation itself) and indirect GHGs (from the value chain) considered?

8. Does the organization adopt sustainable technologies or practices to minimize emissions?

9. Are there any initiatives to raise awareness and train employees about the importance and methods of GHG reduction?

10. Does the company transparently communicate its emissions and reduction efforts to the public and other stakeholders?

Assessing GHG emissions is an integral part of an organization's environmental responsibility. By identifying, measuring, and working to reduce these emissions, companies not only contribute to the preservation of the environment but also align with stakeholder expectations and prepare for a future where sustainability is paramount.

The impact of GHG emissions on the global climate cannot be underestimated. Given the urgency of climate change, it is imperative that organizations take proactive steps to address this challenge. By actively engaging in reducing emissions, companies position themselves as leaders in sustainability, fostering not only a responsible business environment but also a more livable world for future generations. With the checklist in hand, organizations have a valuable resource to guide their efforts in this vital direction.

2.2 - Energy Efficiency and Renewable Sources

In a world of transformation, the search for energy efficiency and the transition to renewable sources has become imperative. The increasing pressure to combat climate change requires organizations to assess their energy utilization, optimize their processes, and consider more sustainable alternatives. This checklist serves as a comprehensive tool for companies to evaluate and improve their approach to energy.

1. Does the organization regularly monitor and record its energy consumption?

2. Are there any targets set for energy efficiency improvement within a specific timeframe?

3. Is the company aware of and compliant with local and international regulations on energy efficiency?

4. Are there systems or technologies in place to optimize energy use?

5. Does the organization invest in renewable energy sources for its operations, or is it considering doing so in the near future?

6. Are periodic reviews carried out to identify areas for improvement with regard to energy use?

7. Is there an organizational commitment to the ongoing education and training of employees on energy efficiency practices?

8. Has the company taken steps to reduce energy consumption during peak periods?

9. Does the organization communicate its efforts and achievements in energy efficiency and the use of renewable energy to its stakeholders?

10. Are there any partnerships or collaborations with external entities to promote or implement sustainable energy solutions?

In the current global scenario, adopting energy-efficient practices and transitioning to renewable sources are not only good for the environment but also good for business. Reducing energy consumption and diversifying energy sources brings economic benefits while positioning companies as leaders in sustainable practices.

In view of the above, companies that proactively engage in energy efficiency and the exploitation of renewable sources are not only reducing their environmental impact but also preparing for a more sustainable future. With this checklist, organizations can begin to assess where they are now and chart a clear path to a greener and more efficient energy future.

2.3 - Water and Waste Management

In a changing world, conscious water and waste management has established itself as a central pillar of corporate sustainability. Water, an essential and finite resource, along with the increasing generation of waste, requires a systematic approach to ensure its responsible use and disposal.

1. Does the organization have clear policies on the efficient use of water?

2. Are there systems in place to monitor and record water consumption in real time?

3. Does the company adopt practices to reuse or recycle water whenever possible?

4. Does the organization have set goals to reduce waste production?

5. Are there established processes for the segregation, treatment and proper disposal of waste?

6. Does the company adopt recycling and/or composting practices to reduce waste sent to landfills?

7. Are there regular audits to assess compliance with local and international regulations on water and waste management?

8. Does the organization have an awareness and training program for employees on the importance of water and waste management?

9. Are there any initiatives or partnerships with external stakeholders to improve water and waste management?

10. Does the organization disclose its performance and goals related to water and waste management to its stakeholders?

In a scenario where natural resources are under pressure and the consequences of poor waste management are evident, proper water and waste management has become a priority for organizations around the world. Effective management of these resources is not only an ethical issue, but also an opportunity for companies to position themselves positively and make a difference.

Adopting robust water and waste management practices brings both tangible and intangible benefits. In addition to direct savings in operating costs, companies that manage these resources responsibly gain recognition and trust, strengthening their reputation. This checklist is a valuable tool to help organizations walk a more sustainable path, ensuring a positive legacy for future generations.

2.4 - Impact on Biodiversity and Ecosystems

In a changing world, the responsible interaction of companies with biodiversity and ecosystems cannot be neglected. Healthy ecosystems are vital to society and the economy, sustaining human life with essential services such as food, water, and clean air. Understanding and minimizing negative impacts on biodiversity is crucial to ensure business resilience and to protect global natural heritage.

1. Does the organization have a clear policy on the protection of biodiversity and ecosystems?
2. Are there environmental impact studies carried out before starting projects in sensitive areas?
3. Are there mechanisms in place to monitor and assess the ongoing impact of operations on local biodiversity?
4. Is the company looking for alternatives to minimize the disturbance of sensitive habitats?
5. Are there efforts to restore habitats that have been previously disturbed or degraded?

6. Does the company collaborate with or support conservation projects at a local or global level?

7. Are there any guidelines to prevent the introduction of invasive species into new environments?

8. Does the organization consider the importance of ecological corridors in its operations and planning?

9. Are there training sessions for employees on the importance of biodiversity and how their activities can affect it?

10. Does the company transparently communicate its actions and impacts related to biodiversity to stakeholders?

We live in a critical period where many species are under threat and entire ecosystems are at risk of disappearing. Biodiversity loss and ecosystem degradation have direct and indirect consequences on businesses, from disrupting supply chains to losing consumer confidence. On the other hand, the protection and active restoration of biodiversity can open up new business opportunities and strengthen the corporate image.

Companies that understand their role in protecting biodiversity and ecosystems and take proactive action not only reduce risks but also better align with societal expectations. This checklist is an indispensable tool to guide organizations on this path, helping them to become agents of positive change and contribute to a more sustainable future.

2.5 - Evaluation of Pollutants and By-Products

In an era of growing awareness of environmental impact, the role of businesses in assessing and managing their pollutants and by-products has become a crucial component of a sustainable future. Recognizing that our industrial and commercial actions can have lasting repercussions on the environment requires a thorough and responsible analysis of these impacts. Given this, this checklist serves as a vital tool for organizations looking to assess their environmental effects, specifically related to pollutants and by-products.

1. Has the company identified and cataloged all pollutants and by-products resulting from its operations?

2. Is there a continuous monitoring system in place to track and measure the release of these pollutants?

3. Does the organization adopt practices to minimize the production of harmful by-products?

4. Are there protocols for the responsible treatment and disposal of pollutants?

5. Does the company have contingency plans in place for leaks or accidental releases of pollutants?

6. Is regular training for employees on the safe handling of polluting materials and substances?

7. Are there initiatives to reuse or recycle by-products whenever possible?

8. Does the organization keep detailed records of the amounts and types of pollutants released annually?

9. Are there efforts to research and adopt less polluting technologies in your operations?

10. Does the company seek certifications or seals that attest to its responsible practices in relation to the management of pollutants and by-products?

Pollutants and byproducts, when not managed correctly, can cause significant damage to the environment, negatively impacting water, soil, and air. In addition to the environmental implications, improper handling of these materials can result in legal and image repercussions for companies. On the other hand, effective management of these elements can not only reduce risks but also bring opportunities. Turning by-products into new products or adopting clean technologies can open up new markets and enhance the company's reputation.

In today's context, it's not just about complying with regulations, it's about staying ahead of the curve by adopting practices that demonstrate a genuine commitment to sustainability. The checklist presented here not only guides companies in this regard, but also reinforces the idea that, by taking care of the environment, organizations are also taking care of their future and the planet as a whole.

2.6 - Environmental Impact Mitigation Strategies

The growing awareness of environmental issues has led companies in all industries to re-evaluate their operations and practices. The mitigation of environmental impacts has become a priority, not only out of responsibility and ethics, but also as a strategic necessity in a world of transformation. Implementing effective strategies to reduce impact is crucial for the long-term sustainability of any organization.

1. Does the organization have a clear plan of action to reduce its carbon footprint?

2. Is there a formalized commitment to invest in cleaner and more efficient technologies?

3. Does the company have programs in place to reduce the waste of resources, such as water and energy?

4. Are there initiatives to increase recycling and reduce waste going to landfills?

5. Does the organization seek partnerships or collaborations with environmental entities or research groups to improve its practices?

6. Are there established and measurable targets for reducing emissions and other impacts?

7. Are there training and awareness programs for employees about sustainable practices?

8. Does the company have a system in place to regularly monitor and report on its progress in mitigating impacts?

9. Is there a plan in place to deal with crisis situations or environmental emergencies?

10. Is there an ongoing feedback and review process to update and improve mitigation strategies?

In an increasingly competitive business environment, adopting effective mitigation strategies not only protects the environment but also confers a competitive advantage on businesses. Those that adopt sustainable practices tend to be viewed more favorably by customers, investors, and stakeholders. Additionally, well-planned and executed strategies can result in significant savings in the long run by optimizing the use of resources and avoiding costs associated with fines or remedies.

Mitigating environmental impacts goes beyond simply complying with regulations. It represents a proactive vision of doing business, where respect for the natural environment is integrated into the core of business operation. As we move forward, it is imperative that organizations recognize the inherent value of our natural world and take decisive action to protect it. This checklist serves as a starting guide, but real change comes with continued action, innovation, and a commitment to creating a more sustainable future for all.

2.7 - Environmental Commitments and Targets

In a global context of constant change and growing awareness of the need for environmental protection, companies and organizations are being urged to set and meet clear targets related to the environment. Not only are these goals indicative of corporate responsibility, but they are also valuable instruments for assessing progress, identifying areas for improvement, and ensuring transparency.

1. Does the organization have a clearly defined formal statement of environmental commitment?

2. Are the environmental goals set in line with international standards or agreements, such as the Paris Agreement?

3. Are there clear and measurable metrics associated with each environmental goal?

4. Has the company implemented systems or tools to regularly monitor progress against set goals?

5. Is there a comprehensive strategic plan that details how each goal will be achieved, including resources and timelines?

6. Does the organization promote internal awareness of commitments and goals, ensuring employee engagement?

7. Are there mechanisms in place to review and adjust goals, based on results and feedback?

8. Does the organization collaborate with external stakeholders, such as local communities or NGOs, in setting or revising targets?

9. Are environmental commitments and targets publicly communicated, promoting transparency and allowing for accountability?

10. Is senior management directly involved and committed to achieving environmental goals?

Organizations that are dedicated to defining, monitoring, and communicating their environmental commitments and goals not only highlight their corporate responsibility, but also put themselves in a favorable position before customers, investors, and society at large. The benefits of taking a proactive approach go beyond reputation; They can include operational efficiencies, innovation, and even competitive advantages in specific markets.

It is vital to recognize that while goals and commitments are crucial, the true value lies in ongoing action and measurable progress. As organizations move forward, commitments should be seen as alive and adaptable, reflecting both internal advancements and changes in the global landscape. This checklist is just a starting point. The journey towards sustainability requires dedication, innovation, and a genuine commitment to making a difference in the world.

2.8 - Carbon Bonding

In a global scenario marked by rapid transformations, it is essential to monitor, manage and, whenever possible, reduce the carbon footprint. In the face of current climate challenges, companies and institutions are beginning to recognize the relevance of assessing the amount of greenhouse gases emitted directly or indirectly by their activities.

1. Does the organization have a standardized methodology for calculating its carbon footprint?

2. Is there a regular system of collecting data related to carbon emissions across departments and functions?

3. Does the company rely on international standards, such as the Greenhouse Gas Protocol, when assessing its emissions?

4. Is there a record of direct emissions from sources owned or controlled by the organization?

5. Are indirect emissions, resulting from the generation of energy purchased and consumed, properly tracked and documented?

6. Does the organization identify and record other indirect emissions, such as those resulting from its value chain?

7. Are mitigation actions, such as the purchase of carbon credits or investment in renewable energy, considered?

8. Are there clear targets set for carbon footprint reduction over time?

9. Are stakeholders periodically informed about the organization's performance and progress in relation to the carbon footprint?

10. Is there a commitment to continuously review and update practices and targets related to the carbon footprint?

The carbon footprint represents an essential metric in the current business context, as it goes beyond the mere measurement of emissions. It becomes a reflection of an organization's commitment to the environment and demonstrates its responsibility to future generations. Effective carbon footprint assessment can lead to a range of benefits, from optimizing processes to strengthening the corporate image.

The challenge lies not only in establishing metrics, but in integrating them into the organization's overall strategy. The climate reality demands concrete actions and strategies. Having a clear view of the carbon footprint allows organizations to proactively position themselves, adapt to regulatory changes, and align with stakeholder expectations. At the end of the day, every step taken towards a more sustainable and balanced world brings benefits not only to the planet, but also to the organization that is dedicated to making a difference.

Chapter 3: Social Approach

3.1 - Corporate Culture Assessment

Amid the constant transformations of the global landscape, corporate culture has become a central element in the operations and strategies of companies around the world. More than just values and missions written on paper, corporate culture is the pulse that dictates the way business is conducted and how people behave within an organization. A solid and positive culture can serve as a guide, directing employees toward a common goal, while a weak or negative culture can cause disunity and a lack of direction.

1. Does the organization have a clear statement of its mission, vision, and values?

2. Are corporate values reflected in the daily actions and decisions of leadership?

3. Are there ongoing training programs for immersion and culture strengthening?

4. Are there open and safe channels for employee feedback on the work culture and environment?

5. Are new employees onboarded and culture-oriented from the start?

6. Does culture promote diversity and inclusion at all hierarchical levels?

7. Is there recognition and reward for those who exemplify and live up to the corporate culture?

8. Are there metrics and indicators used to monitor the health and strength of corporate culture?

9. Is the impact of culture on customer satisfaction and business outcomes reviewed regularly?

10. Do external stakeholders, such as customers and partners, perceive the corporate culture as positive and in line with their expectations?

A strong and authentic corporate culture is not just limited to the inside of the walls of the organization. It permeates every interaction and manifests itself in daily actions and decisions, leaving a lasting impression on customers, partners, and stakeholders. In many cases, it is culture that sets a company apart from the competition, as it reflects the soul and purpose of the organization.

Continuous assessment of corporate culture is vital to ensure its relevance and effectiveness. As the world changes, organizations must adapt, and culture is no exception. Focusing on culture, ensuring that it is alive, breathed, and exemplified by everyone from leadership to grassroots is crucial for long-term success and sustainability. By dedicating themselves to cultivating and nurturing a positive, unified culture, organizations are, in effect, investing in their most precious asset: people. And when people thrive, so does the organization.

3.2 - Health, Safety and Well-being of Employees

In an era of rapid change, attention to the health, safety and well-being of employees has established itself as a cornerstone for globally responsible companies. Committed companies not only meet the immediate needs of their employees, but also proactively invest in practices that ensure a safe, healthy and well-being work environment.

1. Does the organization have clear protocols in place to identify and mitigate occupational hazards?

2. Are there regular occupational health and safety training programmes?

3. Does the company promote wellness initiatives, such as mental health programs and team building activities?

4. Robust systems are in place to report and respond to health and safety-related incidents?

5. Do employees have access to preventive health resources, such as regular checkups and vaccinations?

6. Does the organization periodically review and update its health and safety policies based on legislative or industry changes?

7. Is there a structure in place to support employees who return to work after health issues or sick leave?

8. Are employees encouraged to actively participate in committees or groups focused on health and safety?

9. Is the company committed to keeping employees informed about possible risks in the work environment and preventive measures?

10. Is there an open and anonymous channel for employees to express concerns related to health, safety, and well-being?

Prioritizing employee health, safety, and well-being is more than just an obligation; It's an investment in human capital that ultimately fuels organizational success and resilience. Companies that are actively engaged in proactive practices demonstrate a genuine commitment to their people and consequently reap the benefits of a more satisfied, productive, and loyal workforce.

Constantly evaluating and improving these practices is crucial to staying ahead of the curve in an ever-evolving business landscape. A strategic and comprehensive approach to promoting health, safety, and well-being will ensure that organizations not only comply with regulations but also establish themselves as leaders in their industry. By giving employees the tools and environment they need to thrive, companies are creating an ecosystem where everyone can reach their full potential.

3.3 - Human Rights

In a world in constant transformation, valuing and protecting human rights are essential pillars for responsible organizations. A holistic approach to these rights not only reflects an ethical operation, but also indicates a progressive and visionary leadership that understands the importance of human well-being in the context of business.

1. Does the organization have a clear policy on the respect and protection of human rights?

2. Are there procedures in place to ensure that suppliers and business partners also respect human rights?

3. Is there regular training for staff on the importance and practices of human rights?

4. Does the company have mechanisms in place to identify and prevent cases of discrimination or harassment in the workplace?

5. Is there a transparent and effective process for dealing with complaints related to human rights violations?

6. Does the organization commit to equitable employment practices, ensuring equal opportunities for all?

7. Are there initiatives that promote inclusion and diversity in the workplace?

8. Does the company regularly monitor and assess its impacts on local communities, ensuring that their rights are respected?

9. Are there strategies to minimize the negative impacts of the company's operations in areas with vulnerable populations?

10. Does the organization conduct human rights impact assessments before entering new markets or starting new projects?

Human rights, while universal, need continuous vigilance to ensure that they are respected and promoted. Organizations that integrate strong human rights practices into their operations demonstrate not only ethics, but a vision that understands the interdependence between human well-being and business success.

Integrating a human rights-centric approach is essential to navigating the modern global landscape. By prioritizing the respect and dignity of each individual, companies solidify their position as progressive leaders and ensure a healthy and sustainable relationship with employees, customers, and communities. By setting high standards, they inspire others to follow suit, raising the bar for responsible business practices around the world.

3.4 - Engagement with Local Communities

In a world of transformation, one of the most critical factors for the success and sustainability of organizations is their relationship with local communities. Properly engaging with these communities not only minimizes risk and avoids conflict, but also creates opportunities, strengthens brand image, and builds lasting relationships that benefit both parties.

1. Does the organization have a clear strategy for engaging with local communities?

2. Are there regular consultations with community leaders and members to understand their concerns and expectations?

3. Are there any ongoing programs or initiatives that directly benefit local communities?

4. Does the organization consider the cultural and socioeconomic impacts of its operations on local communities?

5. Are trainings or workshops offered to train community members in areas relevant to the organization?

6. Are there transparent mechanisms in place for the community to express concerns or complaints regarding the company's activities?

7. Does the organization have a local hiring policy or does it support local businesses through its operations?

8. Are there any established partnerships with local organizations, such as NGOs or educational entities, for community projects?

9. Does the organization regularly assess and monitor the impact of its activities on local communities?

10. Are reports or updates published on community engagement and initiatives?

The depth and quality of engagement with local communities can define an organization's success in a specific market. Companies that understand and value the nuances and specificities of each community they interact with are more likely to thrive as they create an environment of mutual cooperation.

True sustainability goes beyond an organization's internal operations. It involves creating an ecosystem where local communities feel valued and seen as essential partners. When companies embrace this commitment, they lay a strong foundation for long-term growth and strengthen their position as agents of positive change. In a world where interconnectedness is the norm, genuine engagement with local communities is more than good practice – it's a necessity.

3.5 - *Diversity and Inclusion*

In times of accelerated transformation, leading companies recognize the crucial role of diversity and inclusion (D&I) in building resilient, innovative, and highly productive teams. Diversity and inclusion are not just contemporary buzzwords, but key pillars that drive business success, fueling vibrant corporate cultures and equitable work environments.

1. Does the company have a formalized diversity and inclusion policy that is communicated to all employees?

2. Are there clear metrics in place to monitor and evaluate progress in D&I?

3. Is the organization's leadership representative of the diversity of the workforce and community?

4. Are diversity, equity, and inclusion-focused training programs available to employees?

5. Does the organization encourage and support affinity groups or networks of employees dedicated to specific D&I issues?

6. Is the recruitment process structured to attract and retain diverse talent?

7. Are there mechanisms in place to avoid unconscious bias during selection and promotion processes?

8. Is there regular and open feedback on D&I issues, allowing employees to voice their concerns?

9. Does the company evaluate its suppliers and partners based on their D&I commitments and practices?

10. Are there support mechanisms available for employees who may face challenges related to inclusion in the workplace?

Investing in diversity and inclusion can transform businesses in many ways. A diverse workforce offers a wide range of perspectives that can fuel innovation, enhance decision-making, and drive better overall performance. When employees feel like they belong and that their voices are heard, they are more likely to feel committed, motivated, and satisfied in their roles.

In a competitive global landscape, companies that take a proactive approach to promoting diversity and inclusion are more likely to attract top talent, meet the needs of a diverse market, and ensure customer satisfaction. Inclusion has become a strategic differentiator, directly impacting companies' reputations, profitability and, most importantly, their legacy for future generations. With the right analytics, organizations can continue to advance their

D&I journey, ensuring a more inclusive and equitable future for all.

3.6 - Training, Education and Professional Development

In a world of transformation, the sustainable progress of a company is intrinsically linked to the ability to invest in the development of its employees. Training, education, and professional development not only enhance individual skills, but also strengthen organizational culture, drive innovation, and solidify the company's commitment to ESG (Environmental, Social, and Governance) standards.

1. Does the organization have a clear strategy for training and professional development that aligns with its strategic objectives?

2. Do employees have regular access to continuing education opportunities relevant to their roles?

3. Are specific training programs available that address environmental, social and governance issues?

4. Is there a system in place to evaluate the effectiveness of training and development programs?

5. Does the organization promote initiatives that encourage lifelong learning, such as scholarships or tuition reimbursement?

6. Are there mechanisms in place to identify and fill skills gaps among employees?

7. Are leaders and managers empowered to support and mentor their subordinates in the development of their careers?

8. Is the commitment to education and professional development communicated and visible at all hierarchical levels?

9. Are employees encouraged to attend external conferences, seminars, and workshops to expand their knowledge?

10. Does the company have partnerships with educational institutions or professional organizations to facilitate the development of its employees?

Progressive companies recognize that continued investment in professional development is a smart strategy for the future. Human capital, strengthened by training and continuous learning, becomes an invaluable asset that drives not only economic success but also a broader positive impact. Integrating robust training and development practices into corporate culture demonstrates a genuine commitment to employee well-being and the long-term sustainability of the organization.

By emphasizing the importance of training, education, and professional development, organizations not only enhance the skills and competencies of their employees but also cultivate inspiring work environments where people feel valued, motivated, and committed to the company's mission. And on a global stage, this emphasis on human development not only strengthens the organization internally, but also positions it favorably in the market, highlighting it as a responsible and visionary leader in ESG practices. Dedication to the personal and professional growth of employees is, without a doubt, a winning strategy for a sustainable and successful future.

3.7 - Management of Complaints and Feedbacks in the Social part

In a changing world, where stakeholder voices gain prominence and power, effective management of complaints and feedback becomes crucial. Organizations, by proactively addressing these voices and responding transparently and responsibly, demonstrate a genuine commitment to ESG (Environmental, Social, and Governance) standards.

1. Does the company have clear and accessible mechanisms in place for stakeholders to express their complaints or feedback?

2. Is there a standardized process for categorizing, prioritizing, and handling these feedbacks and complaints?

3. Are employees adequately trained to handle complaints and feedback in a respectful and effective manner?

4. Does the organization monitor the frequency and types of complaints to identify trends and areas for improvement?

5. Is there a system of accountability in relation to the handling and response of complaints?

6. Does the company have a history of responding transparently and in a timely manner to significant feedback or complaints?

7. Are technological tools or platforms used to facilitate the recording and monitoring of feedback and complaints?

8. Are there periodic reviews of complaint management procedures to ensure their effectiveness and relevance?

9. Does the company actively seek feedback from stakeholders on its complaint management and related processes?

10. Are the results and lessons learned from feedback and complaints incorporated into the company's strategies and operations?

Dedicating yourself to the management of complaints and feedbacks in the social part is more than just a corporate duty; It's a golden opportunity. By actively listening and responding with empathy and effectiveness, organizations not only reinforce their image and trust with the public, but also identify opportunities for innovation, continuous improvement, and strengthening relationships.

Feedback and complaints are valuable tools for companies to evaluate their operations, policies, and approaches. Effective management of these elements not only prevents crises but also sets an organization apart as a leader in social responsibility. As we conclude this section, we reiterate the importance of incorporating the voice of stakeholders into the core of organizational strategy. Ensuring that every voice is heard and valued is a crucial pillar for building a sustainable and equitable corporate future.

Chapter 4: Corporate Governance

4.1 - Organizational Structure and Governance Responsibilities

In a world of transformation, effective governance has proven to be a differential for companies that seek sustainability and responsibility in their operations. A well-defined organizational structure, with clear roles and responsibilities, is a central pillar to ensure that ESG (Environmental, Social, and Governance) principles are embedded at all levels of the company.

1. Does the company have a clearly defined organizational structure that reflects the importance of ESG principles?

2. Is there a team or committee dedicated solely to ESG issues?

3. Do the organization's leaders have defined responsibilities related to ESG initiatives?

4. Does senior management demonstrate visible commitment to the company's ESG objectives and goals?

5. Are there accountability mechanisms in place in case of failures or deviations from ESG principles?

6. Does the organization promote regular training for its leaders and teams on the importance of governance and ESG principles?

7. Are KPIs (Key Performance Indicators) established to assess the ESG performance of leadership?

8. Are employees clear on who their points of reference are for issues related to governance and ESG?

9. Is there transparency and access to information about the organizational structure and responsibilities related to governance?

10. Are governance decisions made collaboratively, involving different parts of the organization?

Governance is not only about how decisions are made but also about how principles and values are instilled in an organization. A robust and well-defined organizational structure, along with clear responsibilities, is the foundation for ESG principles to be practiced genuinely. This is not just a compliance issue, but a strategic necessity for organizations to excel in today's landscape.

Through a solid organizational structure and well-defined responsibilities in governance, companies can ensure that their operations are aligned with the highest standards of ethics and sustainability. In addition, they will be better prepared to face future challenges, respond to stakeholder expectations, and lead positive transformation in business and society.

4.2 - Business Ethics and Integrity

In a world of transformation, the need to solidify ethical values and principles of integrity in corporate structures is increasingly evident. With the rise of environmental, social and governance (ESG) responsibility, companies around the world have prioritized these aspects to strengthen their position and meet the expectations of all stakeholders.

1. Does the company have a clearly defined code of ethics communicated to all its employees?

2. Is there a monitoring and reporting mechanism for ethical issues, ensuring the anonymity and protection of whistleblowers?

3. Is there regular training for employees on the company's ethical and integrity principles?

4. Are the company's suppliers and business partners evaluated for their compliance with established ethical standards?

5. Does the company have a zero-tolerance policy for acts of corruption, bribery, and other unethical practices?

6. Does leadership demonstrate, through its actions, a commitment to business ethics and integrity?

7. Are policies and procedures related to ethics and integrity reviewed regularly to ensure their relevance and effectiveness?

8. Are employees encouraged and recognized for demonstrating ethical behavior in the performance of their duties?

9. Is there clear transparency in decision-making, avoiding conflicts of interest and personal favoritism?

10. Does the company actively seek feedback on its ethical stance and strive to improve based on the feedback received?

In an ever-evolving world, an emphasis on ethics and integrity is not only a response to external demand, but also a vital internal strategy to ensure long-term sustainability and success. A genuine commitment to business ethics and integrity not only minimizes risk but also builds a strong reputation, fosters stakeholder trust, and positions the organization as a leader in corporate responsibility.

Business ethics and integrity are now more than ever crucial to establishing a strong foundation in any organization. Companies that cultivate these values and integrate them into their day-to-day operations have a distinct advantage, ensuring not only compliance but also cultivating a culture that values respect, transparency, and honesty at all levels.

4.3 - Decision Making Mechanisms

In a changing world, the way companies make decisions reflects their commitment to environmental, social and governance (ESG) responsibility. The development of decision-making mechanisms aligned with ESG principles ensures that the organization's actions are transparent, ethical, and future-oriented.

1. Does the company have well-defined processes in place to integrate ESG considerations into its strategic decisions?

2. Are there environmental and social impact assessment tools in place before any significant initiative?

3. Is the company's leadership diverse and inclusive, ensuring broad perspectives in decision-making?

4. Do stakeholders, including employees, customers, and communities, have a say or influence on company decisions?

5. Is there a commitment to regularly review decision-making mechanisms to ensure their effectiveness and alignment with ESG objectives?

6. Do the criteria used to assess leadership performance include their adherence to and promotion of ESG principles?

7. Does the company use ESG-related metrics and performance indicators to inform its operational and strategic decisions?

8. Is decision-making data-driven, ensuring evidence-based analysis and minimizing bias?

9. Is there an accountability system in place for decisions that are not aligned with the company's ESG commitments?

10. Does the company communicate transparently about how and why certain decisions are made, especially those that have significant impacts on stakeholders and the environment?

With a growing awareness of environmental, social and governance challenges, decision-making mechanisms must be up to these concerns. Companies that establish robust and transparent processes not only demonstrate accountability, but also cultivate the trust of their stakeholders. In a rapidly evolving corporate environment, these mechanisms are the foundation for strong governance and sustainable operation.

Embedding ESG principles into decision-making frameworks is a tangible manifestation of an organization's commitment to a more sustainable and equitable future. Adapting to this approach is not only a response to external demands, but a proactive strategy to successfully navigate the contemporary business landscape. With strong decision-making mechanisms, businesses are better positioned to address challenges, seize opportunities, and create lasting positive impact.

4.4 - Transparency and disclosure of information

In a changing world, companies are driven to adopt transparent practices and disclose information effectively. Environmental, social, and governance (ESG) responsibility is grounded in an organization's ability to be open about its operations, impacts, and commitments. This segment focuses on ensuring that transparency and disclosure are consistent with ESG principles.

1. Does the company have clear guidelines for disclosing information regarding its operations, impacts, and ESG commitments?

2. Is there a formal process in place to identify what ESG information is relevant to stakeholders?

3. Does the company publish annual or periodic reports on its ESG performance, which are accessible to the public?

4. Are there mechanisms in place to ensure the truthfulness and accuracy of the information disclosed?

5. Is there a commitment to continuous improvement in the presentation of information, adjusting to the evolving expectations and needs of stakeholders?

6. Does the company disclose information about the ESG risks associated with its operations and how it plans to mitigate them?

7. Are clear deadlines and responsibilities established for the disclosure of relevant information?

8. Does the organization use internationally recognized standards to report on its ESG metrics and achievements?

9. Does leadership actively engage in the disclosure of information, reinforcing the culture of transparency in the company?

10. Is there a feedback channel for stakeholders to express their concerns or suggestions about the information disclosed?

At the forefront of modern business is transparency. Companies that adopt transparent practices and proactively disclose information demonstrate integrity and earn the trust of their stakeholders. In today's business environment, information disclosure is not just a compliance issue, but an essential strategy for creating value and sustaining growth.

Transparency and disclosure of information play a crucial role in building trusting relationships with stakeholders. By establishing clear guidelines, formal processes, and effective mechanisms, companies can ensure that their practices are in harmony with ESG values. Communicating openly about the company's commitments and impacts is a tangible manifestation of its commitment to responsibility and sustainability. Integrating these principles into disclosure practices is vital for companies that want to lead on the global stage.

4.5 - *Management of Conflicts of Interest*

In a changing world, organizations are increasingly under scrutiny for how they manage potential conflicts of interest. Effective management of these conflicts is essential to ensure that corporate decisions are made in an ethical, transparent manner and in alignment with environmental, social, and governance (ESG) responsibility principles. Therefore, a meticulous analysis of the system is essential to understand and optimize the management of these conflicts.

1. Does the organization have clear policies and documented procedures related to identifying and managing conflicts of interest?

2. Are there processes in place to communicate to all employees and stakeholders on how to identify and report potential conflicts?

3. Are periodic assessments carried out to identify areas of risk associated with conflicts of interest?

4. Does the organization keep detailed records of all conflicts of interest identified and actions taken in response?

5. Is there a dedicated committee or team responsible for monitoring and managing potential conflicts within the organization?

6. Does the organization have refusal mechanisms, where individuals refrain from decisions where conflicts may exist?

7. Are there any training programs in place to educate employees on the importance of conflict management and how to handle them appropriately?

8. Are clear deadlines established for reviewing and updating policies and procedures related to conflicts of interest?

9. Does the company proactively communicate with stakeholders about how it addresses and manages conflicts of interest?

10. Does the organization seek external feedback or benchmarking to continuously improve its approach to managing conflicts of interest?

Effective conflict of interest management is not only a best practice, but a crucial necessity in today's corporate landscape. Organizations that adopt robust approaches in this area demonstrate a genuine commitment to ethics and integrity. In addition, the proper management of these conflicts strengthens trust between the organization and its stakeholders, reduces risks, and contributes to building a more transparent and accountable business environment.

The modern business world requires organizations that operate with the utmost transparency and integrity. The ability to identify, manage, and resolve conflicts of interest effectively is indicative of sound corporate governance and an ethical organizational culture. For companies seeking to lead based on ESG principles, proper management of conflicts of interest is not an option, but an undeniable obligation.

4.6 - Rules and Definition of Compliance

In a changing world, the role of compliance in organizations becomes increasingly critical. Being compliant with regulations, laws, norms, and standards is imperative for businesses looking to operate in an ethical and responsible manner. Additionally, the concept of ESG (environmental, social and governance) is deeply integrated with robust compliance practices, ensuring that the company is aligned with the best international standards.

1. Does the organization have a clearly defined code of conduct that outlines compliance rules and responsibilities?

2. Is there a periodic review process for this code to ensure its up-to-date and relevance?

3. Are training standards established for employees on compliance rules and responsibilities?

4. Is there a specific person or team designated to handle compliance issues?

5. Does the organization maintain adequate records to document its compliance with applicable regulations and standards?

6. Are there effective mechanisms in place to report and address compliance violations?

7. Does the company use specific technologies or systems to monitor and ensure compliance?

8. Are internal and external audits conducted regularly to assess the effectiveness of compliance programs?

9. Are the results of these audits communicated to key stakeholders, including senior management and the board?

10. How does the company integrate ESG considerations into its compliance practices and policies?

On the global stage, companies are evaluated not only for their profitability but also for their integrity and compliance. By adopting rigorous compliance practices, organizations demonstrate their commitment to high ethical standards and their willingness to operate in a transparent and fair manner.

A commitment to clear rules and a robust definition of compliance is essential to navigating the regulatory complexity of the modern world. In addition, it lays the foundation for building a corporate culture that values ethics, responsibility, and sustainability. Organizations that excel in their compliance practices are better positioned to earn the trust of their stakeholders, ensuring their sustainability and long-term success. It is this unwavering commitment to integrity and accountability that defines the true leaders of the future.

4.7 - Evaluation and Review of Internal Policies

In a world of transformation, it is crucial for organizations to be dynamic, adapting to continuous changes and ensuring the relevance of their internal policies. By integrating ESG (environmental, social, and governance) principles, companies not only highlight their commitment to sustainability but also demonstrate their determination to stay up-to-date and aligned with global standards.

1. Does the organization have a defined process for the regular evaluation of its internal policies?

2. Is there an established periodicity for the review of these policies?

3. Are the reviews conducted by a multidisciplinary group representing different areas of the organization?

4. Are there documented records of previous revisions, including changes made and justifications for such changes?

5. Are internal stakeholders involved in the evaluation and review process?

6. Are policies reviewed in light of feedback received from external stakeholders, such as customers, suppliers, or regulators?

7. Does the company consider global trends, such as regulatory changes or industry innovations, when evaluating and reviewing its policies?

8. Does the organization seek to align its internal policies with internationally recognized ESG principles and guidelines?

9. Is there a mechanism in place to communicate policy changes to all employees after each review?

10. Does the company assess the impact of these reviews on operational performance and sustainability objectives?

Modern organizations recognize the importance of being proactive rather than reactive. Constant evaluation and review of internal policies not only ensures compliance with standards and regulations, but also drives innovation and operational excellence. Having up-to-date and relevant policies is key to ensuring efficiency, reducing risk, and maintaining stakeholder trust.

The robustness of an organization is not only measured by its ability to create policies, but also by the ability to revise them and adapt them to the evolving reality. By prioritizing the evaluation and review of their internal policies, companies solidify their position as responsible leaders committed to sustainable growth. This commitment to adaptability and accountability reflects a vision of the future in which the organization is prepared to face challenges and embrace opportunities in an ever-changing global environment.

4.8 - Governance Training and Awareness

In a world of transformation, continuous training and awareness of ESG (environmental, social and governance) principles become fundamental for any organization that seeks to align its internal practices with international standards of sustainability and responsibility. Effective governance is not only about setting policies and procedures, but also about ensuring that everyone within the organization understands and is engaged in their implementation.

1. Does the company have regular governance-focused training programs?

2. Is there a structured plan in place to update employees on changes to governance policies and procedures?

3. Are modern tools, such as digital platforms, used for governance training?

4. Are there metrics and indicators to evaluate the effectiveness of the training carried out?

5. Does senior management actively participate in training, demonstrating their commitment to governance?

6. Do the trainings address practical aspects, including scenarios and simulations, to facilitate the understanding of governance concepts?

7. Does the organization hold forums or workshops to discuss and debate issues related to governance?

8. Is there a strategy in place to ensure that new employees are quickly trained and made aware of governance principles?

9. Are the trainings tailored to meet the specific needs of different departments or functions within the organization?

10. Does the company seek feedback from employees after training to continuously improve the training process?

An organization that invests in training and awareness demonstrates not only its dedication to good governance, but also its commitment to cultivating a corporate culture that values transparency, ethics, and accountability. Enablement is not a one-time event, but an ongoing process that must evolve as the organization grows and the global landscape changes.

Cultivating an environment where everyone understands and applies governance principles is crucial to ensure that decisions are made with integrity and that the organization operates sustainably and responsibly. Effective governance training builds a solid foundation for ethical decision-making, strengthens stakeholder trust, and contributes to the achievement of long-term corporate objectives. In the end, what is sought is a prepared, resilient organization aligned with the best global practices of sustainability and responsibility.

Chapter 5: Supplier Evaluation

5.1 - ESG Selection and Qualification of Suppliers

In a changing world, ensuring that a company's suppliers are aligned with ESG (environmental, social, and governance) standards is crucial. This alignment not only ensures supply chain accountability and sustainability, but also minimizes risk and enhances brand value in the global market. If organizations want to achieve ESG excellence, they should consider the ESG qualification of their suppliers as an integral part of their strategy.

1. Does the organization have defined criteria to assess suppliers' ESG practices during the selection process?

2. Is there a structured process in place to periodically assess existing suppliers against ESG standards?

3. Are systems or platforms in place to track and monitor suppliers' ESG compliance?

4. Does the company consider internationally recognized ESG-related certifications during the supplier selection process?

5. Are there protocols in place to deal with suppliers that do not meet or violate established ESG standards?

6. Does the organization encourage suppliers to continuously improve their ESG practices through training or partnerships?

7. Do supplier contracts include specific clauses related to ESG standards?

8. Is there a team or department dedicated to ESG supply chain management?

9. Does the company clearly communicate its ESG expectations to suppliers before establishing a business relationship?

10. Is there a transparency policy that allows external stakeholders to see the ESG standards expected of suppliers?

Selecting and qualifying suppliers based on ESG standards is more than a trend – it's an imperative for responsible business. Suppliers who share a commitment to sustainable and ethical practices not only strengthen the integrity of the supply chain, but also contribute to building a sustainable future.

Achieving high ESG standards requires a holistic approach. It means looking beyond internal operations and ensuring that those who provide products and services are equally committed. In the end, ESG supplier selection and qualification is not only about mitigating risk, but also about seizing opportunities, strengthening business relationships, and building a legacy of accountability and integrity. After all, in an era of transformation, true leadership is demonstrated by an organization's ability to positively influence its entire value chain.

5.2 - Supply chain management with a focus on ESG

In the current global scenario of transformations, it is essential that companies align their supply chain management with ESG (environmental, social and governance) principles. This adjustment goes beyond simple compliance; It represents a strategic vision that can differentiate organizations in the market, increase stakeholder trust, and ensure the long-term sustainability of the business.

1. Has the organization defined clear sustainability criteria for selecting and maintaining suppliers?

2. Are suppliers regularly assessed for their commitment and performance in the environmental, social and governance areas?

3. Are there mechanisms in place to monitor and ensure that suppliers comply with local and international environmental regulations?

4. Does the company promote initiatives or training programs for suppliers on sustainable and responsible practices?

5. Is the supply chain reviewed to identify and mitigate potential risks related to human rights violations or poor labor practices?

6. Does the company have a strategy to promote diversity and inclusion within its supply chain?

7. How does the organization handle the management of waste, emissions, and resource consumption in the supply chain?

8. Is there a clear commitment to transparency, allowing the origin of materials or products to be traced throughout the chain?

9. Is stakeholder feedback considered when making strategic decisions related to the supply chain?

10. Does the organization have contingency plans in place to respond to potential supply chain disruptions caused by ESG challenges?

Integrating ESG practices into supply chain management is not just a reactive measure, but rather a proactive opportunity to foster innovation, improve operational resilience, and create shared value. By strengthening ESG standards along the supply chain, organizations not only protect their reputation and reduce risk, but also position themselves as leaders in corporate responsibility.

Supply chain management, when conducted with an ESG focus, not only reflects an organization's responsibility to society and the environment, but also demonstrates its ability to envision the future. With constantly evolving stakeholder expectations, ESG-centric supply management is a strategic pillar for any company seeking operational excellence and a strong, positive presence in the global marketplace.

5.3 - Continuous Monitoring and Evaluation of Suppliers

In the global scenario of transformations, commitment to ESG (environmental, social and governance) principles has become more crucial than ever. Companies around the world are recognizing that in order to truly meet their ESG goals, it is vital not only to incorporate these principles into their internal operations, but also to ensure that their external network, especially suppliers, is aligned with these guidelines. Understanding this need, a systematic approach to monitoring and evaluating suppliers is essential.

1. Is there a robust system in place for regular reviews of suppliers' ESG performance?

2. Does the organization use specific key performance indicators (KPIs) to measure suppliers' ESG compliance?

3. Are there clear mechanisms for feedback and open communication with suppliers about their ESG practices?

4. Are external audits carried out to validate suppliers' ESG claims?

5. Does the organization have a process in place to address and correct ESG deviations or non-conformities identified during the evaluation of suppliers?

6. Are there incentives or recognition programs for suppliers that exhibit exemplary ESG practices?

7. Does the company have an action plan in case of adverse findings related to a supplier's ESG commitment?

8. Are the results of supplier assessments shared with relevant internal stakeholders, such as procurement or risk management teams?

9. Is there a commitment to continuously improve supplier assessment criteria and processes in relation to ESG?

10. Are there established channels for suppliers to share their best practices, innovations, or ESG challenges with the organization?

Continuous supplier monitoring and evaluation is more than an operational necessity; represent an ethical and strategic commitment. After all, one weak link in the chain can compromise a company's entire ESG integrity. Having an effective system for evaluating suppliers means protecting the organization from risk, strengthening business relationships and, above all, ensuring consistency in ESG promises made to stakeholders.

The process of monitoring and evaluating suppliers, when conducted with integrity and efficiency, not only reinforces the company's position as a leader in ESG practices, but also helps to shape a more responsible and sustainable industry. By demanding high standards not only for itself, but for everyone it does business with, the organization strengthens its network, drives innovation, and contributes to a more ethical and conscious business world.

5.4 - ESG Training and Capacity Building of Suppliers

In an era marked by continuous change, the responsibility of organizations is not only limited to the adoption of ESG practices, but also to the propagation of these practices in their value chain. A successful and sustainable strategy includes ensuring that suppliers, who are essential to the operation of any business, are equally aligned and empowered on these principles. Investing in ESG supplier training and capacity building is not only an ethical duty, but also a strategic initiative that drives resilience and innovation across the supply chain.

1. Does the organization have a structured ESG training program for suppliers?

2. Are training resources and materials accessible, clear, and adaptable for different types and sizes of vendors?

3. Does the company conduct periodic evaluations to measure the effectiveness of the ESG training offered to suppliers?

4. Is there an established platform or communication channel to address questions and feedback from suppliers related to ESG training?

5. Are suppliers encouraged to implement ESG practices and share their achievements and challenges after the trainings?

6. Does the organization recognize and value suppliers that demonstrate notable improvements and commitment to post-training ESG practices?

7. Is there a process in place to continuously update and improve ESG training materials and methods?

8. Is there a proactive approach to identifying emerging ESG training areas and integrating them into the enablement program?

9. Does the company encourage suppliers to replicate ESG training and practices for their own suppliers and partners?

10. Is there a metric or system in place to track the progress and long-term impact of ESG trainings conducted with suppliers?

ESG training and capacity building should not be seen as a mere formality or an act of compliance. They are, in fact, powerful instruments for infusing a culture of sustainability and responsibility, from the largest suppliers to the smallest partners in the supply chain. By empowering suppliers, companies not only raise the standards of their network, but also drive innovation and open up new possibilities for collaboration and mutual growth.

By approaching supplier ESG enablement with seriousness and commitment, organizations reinforce their position as responsible leaders, taking a step beyond merely meeting expectations. They actively shape a business ecosystem that is more conscious, resilient, and prepared for the challenges of the future.

5.5 - Ethical Sourcing Policies

In a changing world, the responsibility of organizations extends beyond their internal operations. Ethical sourcing policies emerge as an essential pillar, ensuring that procurement and business partnerships are aligned with the values of environmental, social and governance responsibility. Companies that adopt such policies not only reinforce their commitment to high standards, but also encourage a more conscious and sustainable value chain.

1. Does the company have clear and documented policies on ethical sourcing?

2. Are policies communicated and easily accessible to all relevant stakeholders?

3. Is there a mechanism in place to ensure suppliers' compliance with these policies?

4. Are there specific criteria that suppliers must meet in relation to environmental, social and governance aspects?

5. Does the company conduct regular assessments of suppliers' compliance with ethical sourcing policies?

6. Is there an accountability system for suppliers who do not meet the established criteria?

7. Does the organization offer guidance or training to help suppliers align with ethical sourcing expectations?

8. Are the criteria and policies reviewed and updated periodically to reflect best practices and developments in the field of ESG?

9. Is there transparency in sourcing operations, allowing for the tracking and verification of the origin of products or services?

10. Is there a stakeholder engagement strategy in place to gather feedback and continuously improve ethical sourcing policies?

Rigorous implementation of ethical sourcing policies goes beyond mere risk management. It's about building a legacy of integrity and promoting a fairer and more sustainable global economy. When organizations choose to adopt such practices, they not only ensure that their own ethical standards are upheld but also encourage positive change across the industry.

Taking an ethical approach to procurement is a tangible demonstration of an organization's commitment to sustainable and fair practices. It is a strategic choice that benefits not only the company, but the whole society. Companies that lead in this field not only protect their reputation and strengthen their business relationships, but also actively contribute to a more promising and equitable future for all.

5.6 - Supplier engagement and feedback

In a changing world, integration and continuous dialogue with suppliers emerge as vital components to ensure sustainability in business operations. Establishing robust supplier engagement and feedback collection practices, aligned with ESG (environmental, social, and governance) principles, increases visibility and accountability in supply chains. Such practices contribute to building stronger, more transparent and effective relationships by helping companies proactively identify and address challenges and opportunities in their supply chain.

1. Does the company have mechanisms in place for regular engagement with its suppliers?

2. Are there clear and accessible channels for suppliers to provide feedback on ESG-related policies, practices, or concerns?

3. Does the organization hold periodic meetings or forums with suppliers to discuss ESG issues?

4. Are there processes in place to review and act on feedback received from suppliers?

5. Does the company recognize and reward suppliers who demonstrate exemplary ESG practices?

6. Does the company have a system in place to track and document supplier engagement and feedback?

7. Is supplier feedback integrated into the organization's ESG strategies and action plans?

8. Does the organization provide resources or support to help suppliers improve their ESG practices?

9. Does supplier engagement consider diversity and inclusion, involving suppliers of different sizes, industries, and geographies?

10. Does the company publicly disclose its efforts and results related to supplier engagement and feedback in the context of ESG?

Deepening engagement with suppliers and valuing their feedback is an initiative that goes beyond simply optimizing the supply chain. It represents a genuine commitment to nurturing more responsible, transparent and sustainable business relationships. By creating a space for the voice of suppliers, companies not only gain valuable insights into their operations, but also strengthen the fabric of trust and collaboration essential to addressing the environmental, social, and governance challenges of the 21st century.

Integrating supplier feedback into corporate strategies demonstrates a proactive and collaborative approach towards sustainability. It reveals an organization that understands the interconnectedness of its operations and recognizes that true transformation requires the cooperation and joint vision of all stakeholders. After all, sustainability is a two-way street, and companies that embrace it in partnership with their suppliers are better positioned to thrive and make a difference on the global stage.

5.7 - Compliance rules in the relationship with suppliers

In times of continuous change, where organizations are more exposed and under scrutiny, it is vital to ensure that supplier relationships are anchored in sound compliance principles. ESG (environmental, social and governance) concepts are gaining increasing importance in the global business landscape, and this is reflected in the need for a more rigorous and structured approach to supplier relationships.

1. Does the organization have clear guidelines for the selection and evaluation of suppliers, taking into account ESG criteria?

2. Is there a supplier-specific code of conduct or guidelines outlining expected ESG standards?

3. Does the company have mechanisms in place to monitor suppliers' compliance with compliance rules?

4. Is there a structured approach to dealing with compliance violations by suppliers, including potential sanctions or corrective measures?

5. Are suppliers regularly trained or educated on the organization's compliance expectations and requirements?

6. Does the company have a whistleblowing or communication channel where irregularities or concerns in the relationship with suppliers can be reported?

7. Does the due diligence process for new suppliers include an in-depth assessment of their ESG and compliance standards?

8. Does the organization conduct regular audits or reviews to verify compliance rules by suppliers?

9. Does the process of renewing contracts with suppliers consider their track record and performance in terms of compliance?

10. Does the company communicate transparently to its stakeholders about the practices and results related to compliance in the relationship with suppliers?

At the forefront of modern business management, integrating compliance into supplier relationships has become more than a mere formality; it's a strategic imperative. By doing so, organizations not only protect themselves from risk but also strengthen their reputation and market positioning. Strict adherence to compliance rules, aligned with ESG principles, demonstrates an authentic commitment to ethical, sustainable, and responsible business practices.

Cultivating supplier relationships based on mutual trust and strict adherence to compliance standards is a clear sign of a company that values integrity and transparency. These practices not only protect the organization from risk but also strengthen its position and respectability in the global business landscape. The future belongs to companies that understand the importance of a clean, ethical, and sustainable business ecosystem. And, in this context, ensuring adherence to compliance in the relationship with suppliers is a decisive step in the right direction.

5.8 - Supplier Action Plans and Continuous Improvement

In a changing world, business dynamics evolve rapidly. Organizations looking to excel must not only adapt but also ensure that their suppliers align with these changes, especially with regard to ESG (environmental, social, and governance) principles. Sustainable practices, social responsibility and good governance become fundamental pillars. In light of this, it is essential to ensure that suppliers are committed to effective action plans and a continuous improvement process aligned with these concepts.

1. Does the organization require its suppliers to present clear action plans to address identified ESG issues?

2. Are suppliers encouraged to set clear and measurable targets related to environmental, social and governance practices?

3. Are there processes in place to monitor the progress and effectiveness of supplier action plans?

4. Does the organization recognize and value suppliers that demonstrate significant progress in their ESG initiatives?

5. Are there mechanisms in place to help suppliers facing challenges when implementing ESG practices?

6. Does the organization consider suppliers' continuous improvement efforts when making contract renewal or business expansion decisions?

7. Are suppliers encouraged to share their ESG best practices and successes with other partners in the chain?

8. Does the organization have mechanisms in place to regularly review supplier action plans and ensure they are updated as needed?

9. Are there open communication channels for ongoing discussion on ESG issues between the organization and its suppliers?

10. Does the organization promote training or workshops to help suppliers understand and incorporate ESG principles into their business?

The relevance of having suppliers engaged in robust action plans and a genuine commitment to continuous improvement has never been more evident. With businesses becoming increasingly interconnected, an organization's success is, in many ways, tied to the performance and commitment of its suppliers.

Fostering an environment where suppliers are not only responsible, but also proactive in their ESG initiatives, is an investment in the sustainable future of the business. Organizations that prioritize and support continuous improvement in their supply chain demonstrate a long-term vision, understanding that sustainable growth is a two-way street. Cultivating relationships with suppliers who share this vision and are equally committed to ESG ideals is vital for prosperity and resilience in an ever-evolving business landscape. Integrating these principles into the core of business operations, including supplier relationships, is the path to a more sustainable and responsible future.

Chapter 6: Financial Assessment and ESG

6.1 - Integration of ESG Risks in Financial Analysis

In times of constant change, financial analysis evolves beyond traditional metrics. Leading companies recognize that the risks associated with ESG (environmental, social, and governance) principles have both direct and indirect financial implications. Integrating these risks into financial analysis is no longer an option, but a necessity to ensure long-term business sustainability and resilience.

1. Does the company have a clear methodology in place to identify ESG risks that could affect its financial position?

2. Do the financial reports include detailed discussions of the company's exposure to ESG risks and their potential implications?

3. Are there processes in place to regularly update the identification and assessment of ESG risks as new information emerges?

4. Is the company's leadership involved in reviewing and considering ESG risks in strategic financial decisions?

5. Does the organization consider ESG risks when determining investments, resource allocation, and other important financial decisions?

6. Does the company have tools and systems in place to monitor, in real time, ESG risks and their impact on financial health?

7. Is there regular training for the finance team on how to incorporate ESG risk considerations into their analysis and decision-making?

8. Does the organization promote transparency in communication about how ESG risks influence its financial decisions to stakeholders?

9. Are ESG risks considered in the development and review of future financial scenarios and business continuity planning?

10. Is there collaboration between finance, sustainability, and governance departments to ensure a holistic understanding of ESG risks and their impact?

When addressing the integration of ESG risks into financial analysis, it is vital to understand that these risks, often intangible, can have tangible repercussions on an organization's financial performance. When ESG risks are overlooked, companies can face challenges ranging from regulatory penalties to reputational damage and loss of investor confidence.

On the other hand, companies that successfully integrate ESG risks into their financial analyses demonstrate proactivity, resilience, and a futuristic vision. In doing so, they position themselves more robustly in the face of adversity and capitalize on emerging opportunities, aligning with a global economy that increasingly values sustainability. This holistic approach not only strengthens the company's financial position but also reinforces its commitment to responsible operation and the well-being of all stakeholders. Companies should see this not just as a responsibility, but as a catalyst for innovation and sustainable growth.

6.2 - The Financial Value of Responsible Investment

In a rapidly changing global landscape, we see a growing movement towards responsible investment. This approach, integrated with ESG (environmental, social and governance) principles, becomes increasingly relevant, indicating that sustainability and financial responsibility are not mutually exclusive, but complementary. Integrating these principles can not only generate value for investors, but also contribute significantly to a fairer and more sustainable world.

1. Does the company have clear metrics to assess the financial return on its responsible investments?

2. Is there a transparent commitment to ESG principles in the organization's investment strategy?

3. Does the organization conduct periodic reviews of the performance of responsible investments compared to traditional ones?

4. Are the long-term impacts of responsible investments on the company's financial health considered?

5. Does the company proactively communicate the financial benefits of responsible investments to its stakeholders?

6. Are there mechanisms in place to ensure that funds earmarked for responsible investments are used with integrity and transparency?

7. Are employees and decision-makers trained on ESG principles and their relationship to financial performance?

8. Does the company constantly seek investment opportunities that align financial return with a positive impact on society and the environment?

9. Is there a clear policy in place to reassess and, if necessary, divest from assets that are not aligned with ESG principles?

10. Does the company consider stakeholder feedback when defining or redefining its responsible investment strategy?

Understanding the intersection between responsible investment and financial value is a task that requires attention and commitment. However, companies that have the ability to deftly navigate this territory often find that their choices not only reflect an ethical conscience but also generate tangible value. As investor expectations evolve and the demand for transparency and accountability increases, the ability to articulate and demonstrate the financial value of responsible investments will become a competitive differentiator.

Thus, by embracing ESG principles in their investment strategy, companies not only reinforce their commitment to a sustainable future but also ensure that their financial trajectory is sound and resilient. The integration of these principles, along with the constant practice of evaluation and adaptation, is key to financial success and creating a positive legacy for future generations.

6.3 - Return on Investment (ROI) in ESG Initiatives

In a scenario of rapid change, the integration of ESG (environmental, social and governance) principles into business strategies has stood out. In addition to meeting a growing demand for more sustainable and ethical practices, businesses realize that aligning with these values can be beneficial from a financial perspective. In this context, evaluating the Return on Investment (ROI) of these initiatives becomes crucial to understanding their effectiveness and value.

1. Does the organization have a clear methodology for calculating the ROI of its ESG initiatives?

2. Are there consistent records of initial investment in ESG projects and subsequent returns?

3. Does the company compare the ROI of ESG initiatives to the ROI of other investments?

4. Is there a periodic review of the ROI of ESG initiatives for adjustments and optimizations?

5. Are the ROI results of ESG initiatives communicated to stakeholders in a transparent manner?

6. Are ESG initiatives that show a positive ROI scaled or replicated in other sectors or units of the company?

7. Does the organization consider both tangible and intangible returns when evaluating the ROI of ESG initiatives?

8. Are clear ROI targets set for each ESG initiative implemented?

9. Is there a team or individual responsible for monitoring and reporting on the ROI of ESG initiatives?

10. Does the company use ROI insights from ESG initiatives to inform strategic and operational decisions?

When addressing Return on Investment in ESG initiatives, it becomes evident that these actions are not only a matter of corporate responsibility, but also a strategic opportunity to generate value. Companies that are able to demonstrate a positive ROI on their ESG initiatives strengthen their reputation in the market, attract more conscious investors, and ensure their long-term sustainability.

Given this, it is imperative for organizations not only to implement ESG practices but also to continuously monitor and evaluate their financial impact. After all, a well-informed, data-driven approach allows businesses to optimize their investments, maximize their returns, and at the same time make a meaningful contribution to a more sustainable and just world. With this integrated vision, companies are positioned not only to thrive in the present, but also to shape the future of their industries and the communities in which they operate.

6.4 - ESG metrics and KPIs in financial performance

In today's global business environment, the intersection between financial performance and ESG (environmental, social, and governance) principles is constantly evolving. In the face of this transformation, it is critical for organizations to incorporate ESG-related metrics and KPIs (Key Performance Indicators) to accurately assess the impact of these principles on their bottom line.

1. Does the company have clearly defined ESG metrics that align with its financial goals?

2. Is there a robust framework in place to collect, monitor, and analyze data related to ESG KPIs?

3. Are ESG KPIs integrated into regular financial reporting and stakeholder communications?

4. Does the organization periodically review its ESG KPIs to ensure relevance and accuracy?

5. Are ESG KPIs used to inform strategic and operational decision-making?

6. Is there an identifiable correlation between performance on ESG KPIs and financial performance?

7. Are the results of ESG KPIs transparently communicated internally and externally?

8. Does the company seek benchmarking to assess the performance of its ESG KPIs against competitors or industry standards?

9. Does the organization use stakeholder feedback to refine its ESG KPIs?

10. Is there adequate training and capacity building for teams tasked with monitoring and reporting on ESG KPIs?

Integrating ESG metrics and KPIs into financial performance is not only an emerging trend but an imperative necessity for organizations that want to thrive in the modern business landscape. These metrics and indicators offer valuable insights that can drive innovation, improve efficiency, and solidify a company's reputation.

Taking a data-driven approach to embedding ESG into financial performance allows companies to identify opportunities and challenges with greater accuracy. They can react quickly to changes in the market, optimize strategies, and ensure long-term sustainability. By staying true to ESG principles and utilizing metrics and KPIs to guide their trajectory, organizations not only improve their own performance but also contribute positively to the world around them. And at the heart of this shift, ESG KPIs, when implemented and managed effectively, play a vital role in creating lasting value for all stakeholders.

6.5 - Sustainable Finance Strategies

In current times, the global transformation we are witnessing converges with an urgent need for financing that is more aligned with sustainable practices. As organizations seek financing alternatives, it is imperative that these strategies are not only financially viable, but also responsible in terms of environmental, social, and governance impact.

1. Does the organization regularly evaluate its financing strategies in light of ESG principles?

2. Are there specific sustainability criteria that guide funding decisions?

3. Does the company consider partnerships with financial institutions committed to sustainable practices?

4. Are the chosen funding sources aligned with the organization's long-term goals regarding sustainability?

5. Does the organization have mechanisms in place to monitor and assess the ESG impact of its financing?

6. Do stakeholder communications reflect the organization's commitment to sustainable finance?

7. Is the company constantly looking for innovations and alternatives in the sustainable finance space?

8. Is the organization considering the possibility of issuing green bonds or other sustainable debt instruments?

9. Is there a team or individual responsible for ensuring that financing practices are aligned with ESG principles?

10. Are the benefits of sustainable finance strategies communicated internally and externally, highlighting their added value?

Achieving sustainable finance practices has proven to be critical for organizations aiming for resilient and responsible growth. Adopting such strategies is no longer a choice, but a necessity. Sustainable finance represents not only a commitment to the financial health of the organization, but also to society and the planet.

It is imperative that organizations recognize the interconnectedness between finance and sustainability. The search for financing that respects ESG principles ensures that organizations are equipped to face future challenges while meeting the growing demands for corporate responsibility. By embracing sustainability-aligned financing approaches, companies not only solidify their position in the market but also strengthen their reputation and legacy. And against a global backdrop of transformation, this commitment to sustainable finance practices is what will distinguish truly visionary companies from those that lag behind.

6.6 - Financial Costs associated with ESG implementation

Amid global change and adaptation, organizations are increasingly feeling the need to align their operations with ESG (environmental, social, and governance) principles. The integration of these principles often involves a review of financial strategies, including assessing the costs associated with their implementation. However, these investments have the potential to offer significant returns in the long run, both financially and reputationally.

1. Has the organization identified and cataloged all direct costs related to the implementation of ESG initiatives?

2. Is there a comparative analysis between the initial costs of ESG implementation and the projected financial benefits in the medium and long term?

3. Are the costs associated with implementing ESG being monitored and adjusted as needed to ensure effectiveness and efficiency?

4. Is there a dedicated financial strategy in place to support ESG actions while ensuring that resources are allocated appropriately?

5. Has the organization considered the tax incentives or subsidies available for ESG-aligned projects?

6. Are there procedures in place to periodically reassess the associated costs, considering innovations or changes in regulations that may impact ESG investments?

7. Have the financial risks associated with non-compliance with ESG standards been identified and quantified?

8. Is there a clear understanding of how the costs associated with ESG influence the company's value in the market?

9. Has the organization sought advice or partnerships to optimize investments and mitigate costs associated with ESG implementation?

10. Does internal and external financial communication reflect a transparent understanding of the costs and benefits associated with adopting ESG principles?

Given the growing demand for transparency and accountability, the costs associated with implementing ESG should not be viewed solely as expenses, but as strategic investments. These investments position an organization favorably, aligning it with global expectations and preparing it for a more sustainable and resilient future.

The implementation of ESG practices, despite the upfront costs, has consistently demonstrated its value in today's corporate landscape. As markets adapt and evolve, organizations that actively invest in sustainable and ethical practices not only strengthen their competitive position but also solidify their relevance on the global stage. In this context, it is evident that the benefits of adopting an ESG-focused approach far outweigh the upfront costs, highlighting the importance of having a holistic and future-oriented vision.

6.7 – Financial Market Opportunities and ESG Growth

In the current global scenario, where changes and adaptations are constant, organizations are focusing on aligning their strategies and operations with ESG (environmental, social, and governance) concepts. With this alignment, new financial opportunities arise, paving the way for sustainable growth. Identifying and taking advantage of these opportunities is vital for companies that want to stand out and consolidate themselves in a market that is increasingly sustainability-oriented.

1. Has the organization identified and evaluated emerging financial opportunities linked to ESG practices in its market?

2. Is there a robust strategy to capitalize on these opportunities while ensuring sustainable growth?

3. How does the firm monitor ESG-related market trends to identify new areas of investment?

4. Is the organization actively looking for strategic partnerships or collaborations to expand its reach in the ESG market?

5. Are the products or services offered in line with the demands of an increasingly ESG-oriented market?

6. Does the organization consider the tax incentives and subsidies available for ESG-focused projects as part of its growth strategy?

7. How are feedback from stakeholders, especially investors, used to shape or adjust the company's approach to ESG market opportunities?

8. Does the organization have a clear understanding of how ESG-related financial opportunities can positively influence its market value?

9. Does the company have mechanisms in place to ensure that investments made in ESG opportunities are generating the expected returns?

10. Are there any established metrics and KPIs in place to assess the success and effectiveness of the organization's approach to ESG-related financial opportunities?

By integrating ESG principles into their financial strategy, organizations not only reinforce their commitment to sustainability but also open doors to numerous opportunities for growth. The demand for sustainable investments is on the rise, and companies that are ahead of the curve in this transition will be better positioned to lead in their respective markets.

In this context, it is evident that the financial opportunities associated with ESG are a crucial pillar for companies seeking robust and sustainable growth.

Embracing these opportunities, monitoring trends, and adapting according to stakeholder feedback not only ensures financial growth, but also strengthens the company's reputation, solidifying its position as a sustainability leader on the global stage.

Chapter 7: Engagement and Communication

7.1 - ESG Communication Strategies

Amid the continuous transformations of the contemporary world, organizations are facing the imperative need to align their operations and objectives with ESG (environmental, social, and governance) principles. A vital aspect of this adaptation is how companies communicate their ESG efforts and commitments to their stakeholders. Effective communication not only reflects transparency but also strengthens trust and creates shared value between the company and its audience.

1. Does the company have a clearly defined strategy for communicating its ESG initiatives and progress?

2. Is there a plan in place to regularly update stakeholders on ESG goals and achievements?

3. Are the chosen communication channels accessible and relevant to the organization's target audience?

4. Does the organization use metrics and indicators to show the results of its ESG actions in communication?

5. Is there a team or person responsible for managing and coordinating ESG-related communications?

6. Is the company looking for feedback from stakeholders to improve its ESG communication strategies?

7. Does the company's communication address both the successes and challenges faced in its ESG journey?

8. Do the annual or sustainability reports incorporate ESG-related progress and commitments?

9. Does the organization promote training or workshops to train its team in effective ESG communication?

10. Does the company use digital tools, such as social media or engagement platforms, to amplify the reach of its ESG messages?

In today's volatile business environment, transparency and integrity in communication have become pillars of trust. Strategically communicating ESG efforts not only demonstrates corporate responsibility but also positions a company as a leader in the sustainability space.

In this way, there is a growing relevance of incorporating robust and transparent communication practices in the ESG field. Through effective communication, organizations can not only highlight their efforts in the sustainability sphere but also establish stronger ties with their stakeholders. The key is to ensure that the communication is clear, consistent, and truly representative of the company's actions, thereby creating an authentic and impactful narrative.

7.2 - Management of Stakeholder Expectations

In an ever-changing global landscape, the importance of properly managing stakeholder expectations has never been more crucial. Modern organizations recognize that success isn't just about achieving financial or operational goals; It also involves establishing and maintaining healthy and transparent relationships with everyone involved in the business ecosystem. In this context, alignment with ESG (environmental, social and governance) principles becomes an essential tool to ensure that the management of expectations is done in a sustainable and responsible manner.

Analysis items on Stakeholder Expectations Management:

1. Has the organization identified all of its relevant stakeholders and does it understand their concerns and interests in relation to ESG?

2. Is there an open and effective channel of communication with stakeholders to understand and meet their expectations?

3. Does the company consider stakeholder feedback when making decisions related to ESG initiatives?

4. Does the organization have a mechanism in place to prioritize the needs and expectations of different stakeholder groups?

5. Are there processes in place to regularly review and adjust stakeholder management strategies in light of changing expectations?

6. Does the organization keep stakeholders informed about its progress and challenges in relation to ESG objectives?

7. Does the company seek to build long-term relationships with its stakeholders, based on trust and mutual respect?

8. Do the company's sustainability reports or other communications reflect the perspective and feedback of stakeholders?

9. Does the company hold regular meetings or forums to engage directly with stakeholders and discuss ESG-related issues?

10. Does the organization commit to acting on stakeholder feedback, demonstrating accountability and adaptability?

Active engagement and effective management of stakeholder expectations can be the difference between success and failure in a world where corporate responsibility is in the spotlight. By understanding and meeting stakeholder expectations, companies not only reinforce their reputation but also ensure sustainable and resilient growth.

Recognizing the complexity and dynamism of stakeholder relationships, it is essential for organizations to develop a strategic and systematic approach to managing their expectations. Incorporating ESG principles into this process is not just a trend, but a necessity. In doing so, companies demonstrate their dedication to sustainability, social well-being, and integrity in governance, laying a strong foundation for the future.

7.3 - Stakeholder Mapping and Prioritization

In a landscape characterized by profound and accelerated transformations, the ability to identify, understand, and prioritize stakeholders has become a vital business strategy. Organizations that recognize and adapt to this dynamism are those that, in the field of ESG, are able to establish effective and transparent communication, as well as meet growing expectations in environmental, social and governance issues.

1. Does the organization have a clear and documented process for identifying its stakeholders at all levels?

2. Is there a structured approach to assessing the relevance and impact of each stakeholder on the company's operations and strategy?

3. Does the company regularly update its stakeholder list to reflect changes in the external and internal environment?

4. Are tools or methodologies used to categorize stakeholders based on criteria such as influence, dependency, and interest?

5. Are there mechanisms in place to ensure that stakeholders with significant impact but no direct voice are properly considered?

6. Has the organization established metrics to assess the effectiveness of its interactions with different stakeholder groups?

7. Are stakeholder feedback and concerns integrated into strategic decision-making?

8. Are the organization's employees trained and empowered to understand and manage stakeholder expectations?

9. Does the company commit to concrete actions based on the information collected during the mapping and prioritization process?

10. Is there transparency and openness to receive criticism and suggestions from stakeholders in the mapping and prioritization process?

Mapping and prioritizing stakeholders is not a static task, but an ongoing exercise in engagement and reassessment. Organizations that engage in this process discover opportunities for growth, strengthen their resilience, and expand their capacity for innovation. This aligns directly with ESG principles, allowing companies to stand out as leaders in sustainability, social responsibility, and good governance.

For any organization striving for excellence in today's landscape, understanding the dynamic terrain of stakeholders is critical. This understanding shapes the direction of efforts, guides decision-making, and highlights the path to positive and lasting impact. Investing in proper mapping and prioritization is undoubtedly a decisive step towards building a sustainable legacy.

7.4 - ESG communication and reporting tools

In a scenario of rapid transformations, communication and reporting tools in the ESG (environmental, social and governance) context have become vital. Companies today are challenged not only to act responsibly, but also to communicate these actions clearly and transparently. ESG reporting provides that communication bridge, and the right tools drive the efficiency and clarity of those reports.

1. Does the organization have a defined framework for ESG reporting, which aligns with recognized international standards and guidelines?

2. Are the communication tools used adaptable to accommodate changes in ESG reporting guidelines and standards?

3. Do information systems ensure accurate, relevant, and real-time data collection to feed ESG reporting?

4. Is there an integration between the various data sources to ensure a holistic and cohesive view in the reports?

5. Does the organization use modern technologies, such as artificial intelligence or predictive analytics, to improve reporting accuracy and efficiency?

6. Are there protocols in place to ensure the confidentiality and security of the information collected and reported?

7. Does the company have mechanisms in place to ensure that its ESG reports are easily accessible and understandable to all its stakeholders?

8. Are communication tools capable of serving different audiences, considering cultural, linguistic and accessibility diversity?

9. Does the organization receive regular feedback from its stakeholders on the effectiveness and clarity of its ESG reporting?

10. Is there an ongoing commitment to the training and capacity building of the team responsible for ESG communication and reporting?

Effective communication is at the heart of any successful strategy, and this is particularly true when it comes to ESG reporting. In today's business world, these reports are more than just a formality; They are a demonstration of commitment, responsibility and transparency. They offer a window into the heart and soul of the company, revealing not only what it does, but why it does it.

By adopting robust and advanced communication and reporting tools, companies not only elevate their game in the ESG field but also strengthen their reputation and trust among stakeholders. This is the information age, and those who communicate effectively, transparently, and responsibly are the ones leading the way. Having the right tools for this purpose is more than a necessity; It is a prerogative for any organization that aspires to excellence in an ever-evolving world.

7.5 - Feedback and Open Dialogue with Stakeholders

In the context of dynamic transformations, open dialogue and continuous feedback with stakeholders become crucial for the alignment and advancement of ESG (environmental, social, and governance) practices. These interactions provide valuable insights that can shape future strategies while solidifying trusting relationships between organizations and stakeholders.

1. Has the organization established formal channels to receive regular feedback from stakeholders on ESG practices and reporting?

2. Is there a clear mechanism in place to ensure that feedback received from stakeholders is evaluated and considered in decision-making?

3. Does the organization hold regular meetings or forums to facilitate open and direct dialogue with its stakeholders?

4. Are there appropriate tools and resources to monitor and document stakeholder interactions and discussions?

5. Does the organization commit to responding to stakeholders' concerns and suggestions within a reasonable timeframe?

6. Are there procedures in place to periodically review and update stakeholder engagement strategies?

7. Are there initiatives in place to educate and inform stakeholders about the organization's ESG practices and their impacts?

8. Are employees trained and encouraged to maintain an open and constructive dialogue with stakeholders?

9. Is there special consideration for vulnerable or marginalized stakeholder groups, ensuring that their voices are heard and valued?

10. Is stakeholder feedback integrated into the organization's strategic planning and ESG practice review process?

In a world where actions speak louder than words, genuine dialogue and constant feedback emerge as the most powerful tools to strengthen an organization's ESG commitment. Stakeholders, whether they are investors, customers, employees, or communities, have a unique and valuable perspective. The ability to listen, understand, and act on these insights can be the differentiator that distinguishes a truly responsible and visionary organization.

Knowing that an organization not only listens, but also values and acts on feedback, can redefine the dynamics of the relationship. This active commitment to open dialogue reflects a deep understanding that, in an ever-changing landscape, the organizations that thrive are those that keep the channels of communication open, building together with their stakeholders the path to a more sustainable and equitable future.

7.6 - Challenges in ESG communication

In a rapidly changing global landscape, effectively communicating ESG (environmental, social, and governance) practices and outcomes is more important than ever. Transparency in communication not only establishes trust among stakeholders but also reflects the organization's commitment to sustainable standards. However, as with any initiative, challenges inherent in the ESG communication process arise that require meticulous attention.

1. Has the organization identified and understood potential obstacles in effectively communicating its ESG practices?

2. Are specific strategies in place to overcome language or cultural barriers when communicating ESG initiatives to a global audience?

3. Does the organization use diverse platforms and channels to reach a wide range of stakeholders while ensuring accessibility?

4. Are constructive feedback and criticism considered to improve the quality and clarity of ESG communication?

5. Does the organization strive to ensure that ESG communication is not only informative but also relevant and engaging?

6. Is there a strategy to combat misinformation or misunderstandings related to the organization's ESG practices?

7. Is ESG communication regularly updated to reflect changes, advancements, and developments in the organization's practices?

8. Do stakeholders have the opportunity to interact and seek clarification on the ESG communication presented?

9. Is there a conscious effort to ensure that ESG communication is not superficial but provides deep and substantive analysis?

10. Does the organization periodically assess the effectiveness of its ESG communication strategies and make adjustments as needed?

Clarity and sincerity in ESG communication are essential to establishing and maintaining stakeholder trust. The ability to identify and overcome communication challenges not only reflects the organization's adaptability, but also its genuine commitment to transparency. In a scenario where sustainability is crucial, organizations must be prepared to face challenges in communication, adopting flexible and receiver-centric approaches to ensure that their ESG message is received, understood, and valued. Acknowledging these challenges and proactively seeking solutions are indicative of an organization that takes its ESG responsibility seriously, not only in action but also in communicating those actions to the world.

7.7 - Communication Improvement Strategies

In an era characterized by dizzying transformations, effectiveness in communicating ESG (environmental, social and governance) practices and results plays a central role. By adapting continuous improvement strategies, organizations not only strengthen their image and relationship with stakeholders, but also demonstrate their adaptability to an ever-evolving world.

1. Does the organization have a formalized plan to optimize its ESG communication?

2. Is there an investment in tools and technologies that increase the effectiveness of ESG communication?

3. Are regular trainings conducted for teams involved in ESG communication, reinforcing best practices and new approaches?

4. Does the organization seek to adapt its language and approach according to different target audiences, respecting cultural and linguistic diversities?

5. Is there a review and feedback process, where ESG communication is evaluated for its clarity, relevance and effectiveness?

6. Do communication strategies incorporate visual media, such as charts, infographics, and videos, to make information more accessible and engaging?

7. Are performance indicators established to monitor and measure the impact of ESG communication?

8. Does the organization foster interactivity and engagement, allowing stakeholders to actively participate in the ESG conversation?

9. Do communication improvement strategies take into account the evolution of media trends and necessary adaptations?

10. Is there an established frequency for reviewing and updating ESG communication strategies, ensuring their continued relevance?

Amid the ever-evolving global landscape, the ability to communicate effectively becomes even more crucial. Adopting robust and flexible strategies to improve ESG communication is indicative of the organization's responsibility and commitment to transparency and quality relationships with its stakeholders. These strategies, when well executed, serve as a bridge, connecting the organization to a diverse audience and expanding its capacity for positive influence. Organizations that are dedicated to improving their communication are, in fact, investing in a more integrated, transparent, and sustainable future.

7.8 - Community Engagement

In a world marked by rapid change, community engagement is a powerful tool for organizations seeking to establish deep and meaningful connections with their stakeholders, taking into account ESG (environmental, social, and governance) principles. Organizations are not isolated entities; They are part of an ecosystem made up of diverse communities. Having a structured approach to community engagement is essential for integrity, resilience, and sustainable growth.

1. Does the organization have a clear strategy for engaging with the local and global community?

2. Are there mechanisms in place to listen to and respond to community concerns and needs?

3. Does the organization regularly monitor and evaluate the impact of its activities on the community?

4. Are there ongoing programs or projects that aim to support and enrich the community, aligned with ESG objectives?

5. Does the organization seek partnerships or collaborations with local groups or entities to enhance its community engagement?

6. Are there resources allocated specifically for community engagement initiatives?

7. Is there transparent communication with the community about the organization's practices, objectives, and results in relation to ESG?

8. Does the organization encourage and support the volunteerism of its members or employees in community activities?

9. Is there a long-term commitment to community development, beyond one-off or occasional actions?

10. Does the organization constantly seek to improve its engagement strategies and practices, adapting to the changes and needs of the community?

In the face of the increasing expectations and responsibilities of organizations in today's society, effective community engagement is more than a best practice; it is an imperative. When executed well, it offers mutual benefits, strengthening both the community and the organization. Through this engagement, organizations not only fulfill their social role, but also solidify their position as responsible and committed leaders. Indeed, when community engagement becomes an integral part of an organization's mission and vision, it creates an environment conducive to innovation, cooperation, and mutual progress, steering us toward a more inclusive and sustainable future.

Chapter 8: Innovation and ESG

8.1 - Integration of ESG into the Innovation Strategy

In a changing world, integrating ESG (environmental, social and governance) into innovation strategy is not only an emerging necessity, but also a valuable opportunity. Innovation is not simply the invention of new products or services, but the ability to recognize and adapt to change while meeting ever-evolving needs. The adoption of ESG principles in innovation strategy enhances positive impact on communities and the environment, while promoting sustainability and long-term growth for organizations.

1. Does the organization integrate ESG considerations into the early stages of the innovation process?

2. Are there established metrics to assess the impact of ESG on innovation initiatives?

3. Does the organization promote the research and development of innovative solutions that address specific ESG challenges?

4. Are stakeholders involved in ESG-focused innovation discussions, providing a diverse and enriched vision?

5. Does the organization have a feedback mechanism in place to assess success and areas for improvement in ESG-aligned innovations?

6. Is there investment in training and continuous training to equip teams with skills and knowledge related to ESG and innovation?

7. Does the organization seek collaborations or strategic partnerships to drive ESG-focused innovation?

8. Do the organization's leaders demonstrate a visible commitment to integrating ESG into the innovation agenda?

9. Are there any recognition or incentive mechanisms for teams or individuals successfully leading ESG-centric innovations?

10. Does the organization regularly assess global trends and developments in ESG to inform and adapt its innovation strategy?

In an ever-changing business environment, those organizations that understand and effectively apply ESG principles in their innovation strategies are better positioned to thrive. By doing so, these entities not only generate value for their stakeholders but also play a crucial role in building a more sustainable and inclusive future. The integration of ESG and innovation represents a powerful fusion of vision, mission, and action – a combination that can serve as a beacon for others to aspire to and achieve on their own transformation journeys.

8.2 - Sustainable innovations in products and services

In a changing world, it is imperative for organizations to stay ahead of the curve by adopting sustainable innovations in their products and services. Integrating ESG (environmental, social, and governance) principles not only strengthens corporate responsibility but also opens doors to new market opportunities and a lasting competitive advantage. With growing consumer awareness and demand for sustainable solutions, companies leading the way with sustainability-centric innovations are shaping the future of business.

1. Does the organization regularly assess the environmental and social impact of its existing products and services?

2. Are there any initiatives underway to develop or improve sustainability-focused products and services?

3. Are suppliers and partners evaluated based on their sustainable commitments and practices?

4. Does the organization consider the full product lifecycle when designing sustainable innovations?

5. Are there clear metrics to measure the success and impact of the sustainable innovations introduced?

6. Does the organization promote transparency by communicating openly about the efforts and results of its sustainable innovations?

7. Is there an active involvement of stakeholders in the process of sustainable innovation, ensuring that solutions meet the real needs of the market?

8. Does the organization invest in research and development with a focus on sustainability to stay ahead of market trends?

9. Are there training and resources offered for teams to stay up-to-date on best practices in sustainable innovation?

10. Does leadership demonstrate ongoing commitment to sustainable innovations, aligning them with the organization's vision and mission?

Companies around the world are recognizing the importance of aligning their innovation efforts with sustainability principles. In doing so, they not only meet the demands of consumers and regulators but also play a crucial role in creating a greener and fairer world. Incorporating sustainable innovations into products and services is not just a passing trend, but a fundamental shift in the way business is conducted. This commitment to sustainability and innovation is what will define the market leaders of the future.

8.3 - Product Life Cycle Assessment

In a changing world, product life cycle assessment (LCA) becomes critical for any organization seeking to align with ESG (environmental, social, and governance) principles. LCA allows for an in-depth analysis of the environmental, social, and economic impacts of a product throughout its existence, from the extraction of materials to their final disposal. This holistic approach helps businesses identify opportunities for improvement, reduce risk, and strengthen their reputation in the market.

1. Does the company perform LCA regularly for all of its key products?

2. Is the data collected for LCA reliable, up-to-date, and based on recognized sources?

3. Does the company adopt internationally accepted standards and methodologies for performing LCA?

4. Are LCA results used to guide strategic and product design decisions?

5. Are there any specific impact reduction initiatives based on LCA's findings?

6. Are stakeholders, including suppliers and customers, aware of the company's LCA practices?

7. Does the company strive to minimize the negative impacts identified during LCA?

8. Is there a framework in place to regularly review and update lifecycle assessments as new information becomes available?

9. Do employees receive adequate training on the importance and methodology of LCA?

10. Does the company proactively communicate its LCA efforts and results to external audiences, including investors and consumers?

Product life cycle assessment is not just a technical tool; It's a powerful statement about an organization's commitment to sustainability. By understanding the full impacts of their products, companies not only respond to rising stakeholder expectations, but also put themselves in a position to innovate and thrive in an increasingly conscious marketplace. True sustainability leadership requires a thorough understanding of the role of products in the larger world, and LCA is an indispensable tool in this process. Organizations that embrace this approach are not only protecting the planet but also strengthening their position in the global marketplace.

8.4 - Circular Economy Initiatives

In the midst of continuous transformations, circular economy initiatives emerge as one of the central pillars for organizations committed to ESG (environmental, social, and governance) precepts. By adopting a model where products and materials are reused, recycled, and regenerated, companies not only minimize their environmental impact but also create sustainable economic and social value.

1. Does the organization have a clearly defined strategy for implementing circular economy practices?

2. Are there processes in place to track and monitor the origin of the materials used in the products?

3. Are the products designed with reusability, recycling or regeneration in mind at the end of their useful lifecycle?

4. Are there any partnerships or collaborations with suppliers to promote circular economy practices?

5. Are there initiatives to reduce the waste of resources and promote efficiency at all stages of the production chain?

6. Does the organization encourage and train its employees on the importance of the circular economy?

7. Is there a commitment to transparency and communication on circular economy efforts and results?

8. Does the company consider feedback from stakeholders, such as customers and local communities, in its circular initiatives?

9. Are there metrics and indicators in place to measure the progress and effectiveness of circular economy initiatives?

10. Does the organization constantly seek innovations and technological solutions that support the implementation of the circular economy?

The focus on circular economy highlights an evolution in the way companies view their products and processes. It's a move beyond traditional sustainability, looking at how businesses can regenerate and create systems that benefit not only the organization, but also society and the environment. By adopting such practices, companies position themselves at the forefront of responsible innovation, demonstrating not only their corporate responsibility but also their commitment to a more resilient and equitable future. The circular economy is not just a trend but an imperative for organizations looking to lead in an ever-evolving global marketplace. By integrating these principles into their strategy, companies can uncover new opportunities, strengthen relationships with stakeholders, and ensure their relevance in the future.

8.5 - Partnerships and Collaborations for ESG Innovation

Amid rapid global transformations, the need for sustainable innovation has never been more crucial. Companies that lead in environmental, social, and governance (ESG) responsibility understand the importance of partnerships and collaborations. Joining forces with other organizations, academia, and communities can accelerate the development and implementation of innovative ESG solutions, fostering broader and deeper positive impact.

1. Does the company have a defined strategy for establishing partnerships focused on ESG innovation?

2. Is there a process in place to identify and evaluate potential partners or employees aligned with the company's ESG goals?

3. Has the organization already established collaborations with academic institutions or research centers to drive ESG innovations?

4. Are there cooperation or partnership agreements with NGOs or other companies focused on specific ESG challenges?

5. Does the organization have mechanisms in place to ensure that the partnerships established are aligned with its values and ethical principles?

6. Are there regular meetings with partners and collaborators to assess the progress and impact of joint initiatives?

7. Does the company encourage co-creation and sharing of ideas among its employees and partners?

8. Is there a commitment to transparent communication about the results and impacts of ESG collaborations?

9. Are there established metrics to assess the success and effectiveness of ESG partnerships and collaborations?

10. Does the company continuously seek to expand its network of collaborations, exploring new opportunities to promote ESG innovation?

Partnerships and collaborations have become essential tools for companies that want to go further in their ESG initiatives. By combining skills, knowledge, and resources, organizations can overcome complex challenges and co-create innovative solutions that have the potential to transform entire industries. These collaborations, when well managed and aligned with a clear vision, can be the key to unlocking new opportunities, reducing risk, and maximizing positive impact.

Recognizing the importance of ESG partnerships and collaborations is a vital step for businesses that want to thrive and lead in today's global landscape. In an increasingly interconnected business environment, those that embrace collaboration and co-creation not only strengthen their position in the market but also contribute significantly to a more sustainable and equitable world.

8.6 - Challenges and opportunities in sustainable innovation

In the global scenario of transformations, the commitment to sustainable innovation is highlighted. This commitment not only reflects an organization's dedication to environmental, social, and governance (ESG) principles, but also its ability to face challenges and seize opportunities along the way. As businesses seek to create a positive impact, it is vital to recognize the challenges and opportunities that emerge on the path to sustainable innovation.

1. Does the company identify and document the key challenges faced in its sustainable innovation journey?

2. Is there a robust strategy in place to mitigate these challenges while ensuring ESG goals are met?

3. Does the organization have a mechanism in place to monitor emerging trends that may represent opportunities for sustainable innovation?

4. Are internal debates promoted to identify and overcome obstacles in the implementation of sustainable practices?

5. Does the organization invest in research and development aimed at sustainable innovation?

6. Are strategic partnerships established to seize opportunities and address challenges in sustainable innovation?

7. Are employees encouraged and empowered to identify opportunities and solutions to ESG challenges?

8. Is there an open channel to receive feedback from stakeholders on potential challenges and opportunities in sustainable innovation?

9. Does the company regularly evaluate the impact and results of its initiatives, adjusting its strategy as needed?

10. Is there a recognition and celebration of sustainable achievements and innovations, even in the face of challenges?

Embracing sustainable innovation requires more than just goodwill; It demands vision, perseverance, and adaptability. Challenges are inevitable, but they are also valuable indicators for learning and growth. Opportunities, on the other hand, show promising avenues that, when exploited effectively, can lead to significant realizations in terms of positive impact.

Recognizing the inestimable value of sustainable innovation, it is essential that companies are equipped not only to identify challenges and opportunities, but also to act on them. This action can take the form of ongoing research, strategic collaborations, or investments in emerging technologies. The essence, however, lies in the company's ability to remain resilient, adaptable, and focused on its commitment to a more sustainable and equitable future. Those who have mastered the art of turning challenges into opportunities are best positioned to lead in an ever-evolving global landscape and make a difference in the world of tomorrow.

8.7 - Goals and Results in ESG Innovations

In the midst of global transformations, setting and achieving clear targets in environmental, social, and governance (ESG) innovations becomes imperative. Leading organizations recognize that having tangible, measurable goals leads to real progress and lasting impact. The importance of aligning such goals with the company's overall vision and of periodically evaluating the results achieved cannot be underestimated.

1. Does the organization have ESG goals that are clearly defined and aligned with its mission and vision?

2. Is there an established timeline for achieving these goals?

3. Does the company use specific metrics to measure progress against these goals?

4. Are the results achieved regularly communicated to internal and external stakeholders?

5. Is there a periodic review of the goals to ensure their relevance and continued effectiveness?

6. Does the organization integrate past feedback and learnings when setting new ESG goals?

7. Do the teams have the necessary resources, including training and tools, to achieve the goals set?

8. Are there accountability mechanisms in place to ensure that targets are met?

9. Does the company recognize and celebrate the milestones achieved on the path to achieving its ESG goals?

10. Are goals and outcomes used as drivers for new innovations and continuous improvements in ESG practices?

Setting robust and measurable goals in the ESG context provides clear direction and purpose for organizations. It acts as a compass, guiding businesses through complexities and ensuring that actions taken align with a larger vision. When executed well, these goals trigger a range of benefits, from improved brand reputation to a tangible positive impact on the world.

However, simply setting goals is not enough. True excellence lies in a company's ability to pursue, achieve, and even exceed these goals. By periodically evaluating results, companies not only measure their progress but also identify areas of opportunity for continuous innovation.

As we move forward, the integration of clear goals and a regular assessment of outcomes in ESG innovations will be key. This helps ensure that organizations not only talk about change but also implement it effectively. Those who embrace this results-centric approach are uniquely positioned to lead into the future by creating a legacy of positive impact and sustainable innovation.

Chapter 9: Monitoring and Continuous Review

9.1 - ESG Monitoring Tools and Techniques

In the midst of global transformations, the tools and techniques used to monitor Environmental, Social, and Governance (ESG) criteria are vital for companies to maintain integrity, accountability, and transparency. Commitment to sustainability and business ethics largely depends on how organizations implement, monitor, and evaluate their ESG practices.

1. Does the company adopt advanced technological solutions to collect and analyze ESG data in real-time?

2. Are there processes in place to validate the accuracy of the data collected?

3. Does the organization use globally recognized benchmarks to compare and evaluate its ESG performance?

4. Is there integration between different departments for collecting and sharing ESG-related information?

5. Are there protocols in place for periodic review and updating of the tools used, ensuring their continued relevance?

6. Does the organization provide regular training to ensure that employees are able to properly use monitoring tools and techniques?

7. Do the monitoring techniques adopted allow the identification of trends and patterns, facilitating strategic decision-making?

8. Do stakeholders have transparent access to ESG monitoring results, promoting trust and engagement?

9. Does the organization use stakeholder feedback to continuously improve its monitoring tools and techniques?

10. Does the company maintain a commitment to exploring new emerging tools and techniques in the field of ESG monitoring?

Accurate and effective monitoring of ESG criteria is a crucial part of corporate responsibility in today's landscape. Companies that adopt advanced tools and effective techniques not only demonstrate their seriousness towards sustainability and ethics, but also strengthen their position in the market. Through robust monitoring, organizations can identify opportunities for improvement, mitigate risks, and strengthen the trust of their stakeholders.

The continuous evolution of tools and techniques, combined with the ability to adapt to changes and emerging needs, will put companies at the forefront of ESG practices. Those that approach monitoring with diligence and innovation will excel, raising their standards and, consequently, the standard of the industry as a whole. The accountability, transparency, and efficiency that come with effective monitoring chart the path to a more sustainable and ethical business future.

9.2 - The Importance of Review and Continuous Improvement

In an ever-changing global context, review and continuous improvement become crucial for companies committed to Environmental, Social and Governance (ESG) criteria. This commitment transcends mere compliance, aligning with practices that notably highlight organizations in terms of sustainability and business ethics.

1. Does the organization have a formalized process in place to regularly review its ESG policies and practices?

2. Are there established performance indicators that guide reviews and continuous improvement decisions?

3. Is there a defined timetable for conducting internal audits aimed at reviewing ESG practices?

4. Does the company engage with stakeholders to get feedback and integrate their perspectives into reviews?

5. Are the results of the reviews communicated internally and externally, ensuring transparency?

6. Are the identified areas of improvement transformed into concrete actions with clear deadlines?

7. Does the organization set clear goals for continuous improvement in relation to ESG?

8. Are the tools and technologies used in the review updated to reflect best practices?

9. Is there a commitment from leadership to promote a culture of review and continuous improvement in ESG?

10. Does the organization regularly compare its ESG performance to that of competitors or market benchmarks to identify areas for improvement?

Continuously reviewing and improving is not only a strategy to meet external expectations, but also a way to reinforce internal commitment to ESG excellence. As organizations integrate these practices, they solidify their position in the market and strengthen the trust of their stakeholders. In addition, they become more agile, ready to adapt to new demands and challenges that arise.

In a competitive business environment, review and continuous improvement are more than recommended actions; are imperative. They ensure that organizations not only meet current standards but also anticipate future trends and emerging demands. The real value of staying up-to-date and constantly seeking improvement lies in an organization's ability to be resilient, adaptable, and truly committed to sustainability and ethics. Consequently, the benefits of such an approach are felt in all facets of the business, from customer and employee satisfaction to profitability and brand reputation.

9.3 - Benchmarking and Peer Comparison

In an ever-evolving global landscape, benchmarking and peer comparison become indispensable for organizations striving for excellence in Environmental, Social, and Governance (ESG) criteria. Through this comparative analysis, businesses can identify gaps in their practices, uncover new trends and innovations, and, most crucially, set realistic and achievable goals.

1. Does the organization regularly identify its key competitors or peers for ESG benchmarking purposes?

2. Are there any defined metrics that are used to compare the company's performance to that of its peers?

3. Does the company have access to up-to-date ESG data and reports from its competitors or peers?

4. Does the organization consider market-leading practices when defining its ESG goals and strategies?

5. Is peer comparison used to identify areas of improvement and opportunities for innovation?

6. Is there a structured process to incorporate learnings from benchmarking into the company's ESG practices and policies?

7. Does the company communicate its strengths and make adjustments based on areas where it lags behind its peers?

8. Are benchmarking results shared with relevant stakeholders to promote transparency and engagement?

9. Is leadership involved and committed to using benchmarking as a tool for continuous improvement?

10. Does the organization have a proactive approach to staying informed about ESG best practices in the industry and beyond?

Benchmarking and peer-to-peer comparison are not limited to maintaining a competitive position; represent a continuous search for improvement. By understanding where an organization stands in relation to its peers, it can set clearer goals, quickly identify areas of opportunity, and make more informed decisions. Additionally, by taking a data-driven, peer-to-peer approach, companies reinforce their commitment to ESG transparency, accountability, and innovation.

The true essence of benchmarking and peer-to-peer comparison is to create a cycle of learning and adaptation. At a time when ESG standards are rapidly evolving and stakeholder pressure is growing, the ability to adapt and evolve is more crucial than ever. In this context, organizations that effectively employ these practices not only maintain their relevance but also position themselves as leaders, shaping the future of sustainable and responsible business.

9.4 - Organizational Feedback and Learning

In a dynamic and ever-changing landscape, organizational feedback and learning become critical for any entity that sets out to truly embrace Environmental, Social, and Governance (ESG) criteria. By cultivating a culture of continuous feedback and learning, organizations are better positioned to adapt, evolve, and lead in the field of ESG.

1. Does the organization have effective mechanisms in place to collect feedback from internal and external stakeholders on its ESG initiatives and practices?

2. Is there a systematic process for analyzing and categorizing ESG-related feedback received?

3. Are technological tools and platforms used to facilitate the collection, analysis, and implementation of feedback?

4. Is the feedback collected periodically reviewed by multidisciplinary teams to ensure a holistic view?

5. Does the organization incorporate learnings from feedback into its ESG strategy and objectives?

6. Are the organization's leaders committed to the idea of continuous learning, using feedback as a valuable tool?

7. Are there regular review and training sessions to disseminate learnings and best practices from feedback?

8. Does the company have indicators or metrics that measure the effectiveness of its actions based on feedback?

9. Are there open and safe channels for employees and other stakeholders to voice ESG-related concerns or suggestions?

10. Does the organization celebrate and recognize teams or individuals who demonstrate an excellent ability to adapt and learn from feedback?

Collecting, understanding, and implementing feedback is not just an exercise in listening; It is indicative of the organization's commitment to continuous improvement. Feedback provides valuable insights by showing the areas that need attention and highlighting where existing practices are making a difference. The true value of feedback lies in the organization's ability to turn it into concrete actions that drive ESG excellence.

The business world recognizes that growth and adaptation are essential for long-term sustainability. By incorporating feedback and fostering a culture of organizational learning, entities not only reinforce their commitment to ESG standards, but also strengthen their positioning as responsible and innovative leaders. This ongoing commitment to improvement and adaptability is what distinguishes truly exceptional organizations and prepares them for the challenges and opportunities of the future.

9.5 - Carbon Footprint Monitoring

In a globalized environment where concern about climate change and sustainability is growing, carbon footprint monitoring becomes an essential tool for companies that want to align with Environmental, Social, and Governance (ESG) principles. Understanding and managing carbon emissions is key to demonstrating environmental responsibility and ensuring conscious performance in the market.

1. Does the company have a robust system in place to collect data on its direct and indirect carbon emissions?

2. Is there a team or department dedicated to managing and reducing the carbon footprint?

3. Are internationally recognized methodologies used to calculate the carbon footprint?

4. Has the organization set clear and measurable targets for reducing its emissions in the short, medium and long term?

5. Are there any partnerships or collaborations with external entities for validation and verification of reported emissions?

6. Does the company invest in technologies and practices aimed at energy efficiency and emission reduction?

7. Are suppliers and partners assessed for their carbon footprint and sustainable practices?

8. Does the organization transparently communicate its emissions, reduction efforts, and progress made to its stakeholders?

9. Is there a response plan in place for carbon-related incidents, such as leaks or unplanned emissions?

10. Does the company seek to offset its emissions through initiatives such as reforestation, investment in clean energy or purchase of carbon credits?

Monitoring and managing the carbon footprint is not only an ethical obligation, but a smart strategy for organizations that want to thrive in a green economy. The commitment to reducing emissions signals a vision of the future, adaptability and a recognition of the demands of an increasingly conscious market.

Environmental responsibility, represented by the monitoring and management of the carbon footprint, is a central pillar of the commitment to ESG criteria. Organizations that engage in this monitoring are not only protecting the planet, but also positioning themselves as leaders in sustainability and innovation. It is this kind of vision and action that will shape the future of business and ensure continued resilience and success in an evolving global landscape.

9.6 - ESG Performance Assessment

The advancement of sustainability in the global business scenario has led organizations to adapt their strategies and operations, aligning them with Environmental, Social and Governance (ESG) principles.

In this context of transformations, ESG performance assessment not only validates current practices, but also guides future decision-making, ensuring a lasting positive impact.

1. Does the company have clear and measurable metrics related to ESG performance?

2. Is there a regular process for collecting, analyzing, and reviewing these metrics?

3. Are the assessment results compared to industry benchmarks or standards?

4. Is there a leadership involvement in the ESG performance evaluation and review process?

5. Are the results communicated to stakeholders in a transparent and regular manner?

6. Does the company consider external feedback, such as from customers or shareholders, in evaluating its performance?

7. Are opportunities for improvement identified and corrective actions based on results established?

8. Is there an integration of the results of the ESG performance assessment into the company's overall strategies and objectives?

9. Does the organization constantly update itself on new global ESG practices and standards?

10. Is there investment in training and training of the team to ensure an accurate assessment in line with trends?

The effectiveness of ESG performance assessment lies in the organization's ability to translate results into concrete actions. It is a continuous exercise of self-knowledge and evolution, which highlights achievements and illuminates areas that require attention and transformation.

Organizations that strive for excellence in ESG performance are those that recognize sustainability as a driving force. Evaluating, adjusting, and evolving are key steps in ensuring that sustainability is deeply ingrained in the culture and operations. In this way, businesses not only ensure a positive impact on the world but also solidify their position as leaders and innovators on the global stage. With regular assessment, organizations have the chance to shape, adapt, and grow in tune with a world that increasingly values ESG commitment.

9.7 - Identification and treatment of non-conformities

In the intricate scenario of transformations involving Environmental, Social and Governance (ESG) guidelines, organizations must be prepared to identify and address non-conformities that may arise. These are deviations or failures to meet the established requirements, which can negatively affect the organization's performance in the ESG pillars. Taking a keen look at these aspects is vital to align practices, correct routes, and ensure that sustainable goals are achieved.

1. Does the company have a structured method for detecting non-conformities in the areas of Environmental, Social and Governance?

2. Is there a team or person responsible for analyzing and handling these non-conformities?

3. Does the organization implement corrective actions in response to identified nonconformities?

4. Are identification methods reviewed and updated periodically to ensure their effectiveness?

5. Is there an organized record of non-conformities detected and actions taken?

6. Are employees trained and made aware of the importance of detecting and dealing with non-conformities?

7. Does the organization use tools or software to assist in identifying and managing nonconformities?

8. Is there an after-action review process to ensure that non-conformities have been adequately addressed?

9. Are stakeholders informed about how non-conformities are handled?

10. Does the company analyze trends and patterns in non-conformities to prevent recurrences?

Proactive identification and proper handling of non-conformities is an essential component for companies that aspire to high ESG performance. Non-conformities can arise as challenges, but by addressing them effectively, organizations turn them into opportunities. Opportunities to learn, realign, and demonstrate genuine commitment to ESG best practices.

Addressing non-conformities is not just a matter of remediation, but a strategy that drives organizational resilience. By prioritizing this process, companies strengthen their integrity, increase stakeholder trust, and solidify their reputation in the market. The conscious approach to identifying and addressing non-conformities demonstrates maturity and commitment to building a sustainable and responsible future.

9.8 - Planning of Corrective Actions

In a world of transformation, companies are continuously challenged to align their operations and strategies with Environmental, Social and Governance (ESG) principles. This alignment often requires the implementation of corrective actions to address deviations, failures, or non-conformities. Efficient planning of these actions is crucial to ensure that problems are solved in a sustainable manner, leveraging the organization's ESG performance.

1. Does the organization have a structured process in place to identify the need for corrective actions based on ESG principles?

2. Is there a team or individual designated to lead the planning and execution of corrective actions?

3. Are corrective action plans documented, including description of non-compliance, root cause, proposed action, and deadlines?

4. Is there a process in place to review and approve corrective action plans prior to their implementation?

5. Are indicators or metrics established to monitor the effectiveness of the corrective actions implemented?

6. Does the organization engage with relevant stakeholders when planning corrective actions?

7. Is there a feedback mechanism in place to learn from corrective actions and continuously improve the process?

8. Are the necessary resources (financial, human, technological) allocated appropriately to ensure the effective implementation of corrective actions?

9. Does the organization communicate internally and externally about planned corrective actions and their progress?

10. Is there a periodic review of corrective action plans to ensure they remain relevant and effective?

Meticulous corrective action planning is a concrete manifestation of a company's commitment to ESG excellence. By proactively addressing non-conformities and implementing actions to correct them, organizations not only comply with regulatory requirements or standards but also demonstrate accountability and transparency.

At the end of the study of this component, it is worth noting that well-planned corrective actions are more than mere compliance exercises. They reflect an organizational culture that values continuous improvement, accountability, and a commitment to high standards. Organizations that approach this planning seriously are better positioned to meet challenges, adapt to change, and thrive in the ever-evolving global landscape. In every corrective action, we see an opportunity to grow, enhance, and strengthen the ESG values that guide companies towards a more sustainable and equitable future.

Chapter 10: Conclusion and Future Vision

10.1 - Future Commitments and Strategic Planning

In a world of transformation, the effective integration of Environmental, Social and Governance (ESG) principles into the strategic planning and future commitments of organizations has become imperative. Responsible conduct of business operations, aligned with ESG values, not only strengthens the corporate image, but also foundations the organization on a sustainable basis, preparing it for the challenges of tomorrow.

1. Does the organization's strategic planning incorporate clear goals and objectives related to ESG principles?

2. Is there an established process in place to regularly review and update strategic planning, taking into account ESG trends and changes?

3. Has the organization identified and documented ESG-related risks and opportunities in its future plans?

4. Is the organization's commitment to ESG principles communicated in a clear and transparent manner to internal and external stakeholders?

5. Does the organization have mechanisms in place to ensure that ESG commitments are monitored and progress is measured?

6. Are leaders and decision-makers adequately informed and educated about the nuances of ESG to make strategic decisions?

7. Does the organization consider stakeholder feedback when formulating and reviewing its strategic planning in relation to ESG?

8. Is there an interdepartmental collaboration in the organization to integrate ESG principles into all aspects of planning?

9. Has the organization established partnerships or collaborations to strengthen its strategic approach to ESG?

10. Does the organization have a post-implementation review mechanism in place to assess the success of its ESG commitments and adjust its course as needed?

As they look to the future horizon, forward-thinking companies understand the importance of integrating ESG into their plans. It is essential not only to ensure sustainability and accountability, but also to drive innovation, adaptability, and long-term growth.

At the end of this section, it is critical to underline that incorporating ESG principles into strategic planning and future commitments is not an option, but a necessity. It is a demonstration of an organization's foresight and adaptability, signaling its maturity and accountability. Organizations that take this proactive path are those that will leave an indelible mark on the world, shaping a future that resonates with sustainability, fairness, and innovation. With each strategic decision, there is an opportunity to reaffirm ESG values, leading the organization to high levels of excellence and impact.

10.2 - The evolution of ESG concepts and emerging trends

In a world of transformation, the concepts of Environmental, Social and Governance (ESG) are no longer the same as they were a decade ago. Organizations face a constant challenge to keep up with and adapt to evolving ESG standards and emerging trends shaping the sustainable business landscape. To stay ahead of the curve and ensure a proactive approach, it is vital for organizations to conduct a regular audit to assess the relevance and effectiveness of their ESG practices.

1. Does the organization regularly monitor changes in ESG guidelines and standards?

2. Is there a system in place to quickly integrate new ESG trends into the organization's operations and strategies?

3. How does the organization identify and act on new opportunities arising from emerging trends in ESG?

4. Is there an ongoing training process in place to ensure staff are up-to-date on the latest developments in ESG?

5. Does the organization have communication channels in place to share ESG insights and updates with its stakeholders?

6. Is the organization's leadership committed to adapting to changes and innovations in the ESG field?

7. Are review and feedback mechanisms in place to ensure ESG practices are relevant and up-to-date?

8. How does the organization validate its position in relation to competitors with regard to the evolution of ESG concepts?

9. Do the organization's ESG reports and disclosures reflect the latest advancements and emerging trends in the field?

10. Is there a proactive strategy in place to anticipate future ESG changes and prepare the organization for them?

ESG principles are dynamic, and an organization's ability to adapt to these dynamics will determine its long-term success. Emerging trends in ESG are not just challenges; They represent opportunities for innovation, growth, and strengthening corporate reputation.

In the context of constant change, success is not only defined by adaptation, but also by anticipation. Organizations that can predict the evolution of ESG concepts are the ones that will shape the future of sustainable business. By recognizing the importance of evolving and emerging trends in ESG, companies not only ensure their relevance but also demonstrate their leadership and commitment to a better world. Adapting to ESG changes is a demonstration of resilience and forward-thinking, preparing the organization to thrive in an ever-changing business landscape. Every update, every innovation, and every step taken toward a more advanced ESG reinforces the organization's commitment to sustainability, ethics, and responsibility.

10.3 - The role of corporations in the sustainable future

In the context of rapid global change, recognizing the role of corporations in the sustainable future becomes critical. The analysis of corporate practices from the perspective of ESG (Environmental, Social and Governance) concepts can shed light on how companies are positioning themselves to contribute to a more responsible and resilient world.

1. How does the organization integrate sustainable practices into its long-term strategy and vision?

2. Are there clear goals related to the environment, such as reducing carbon emissions and conserving resources?

3. Is the organization committed to social practices such as diversity, inclusion, and community development?

4. How does company governance ensure adherence to ethical standards and transparency in operations?

5. Are there initiatives to promote sustainable innovation in products, services or processes?

6. Is the organization looking for strategic partnerships to strengthen its approach to sustainability?

7. How does the company communicate with stakeholders about its ESG efforts and accomplishments?

8. Are there any established metrics and indicators in place to monitor and evaluate progress against ESG goals?

9. Does the organization encourage the training and training of its staff in sustainable and responsible practices?

10. Are there policies in place to anticipate sustainability-related risks and challenges in the future?

Corporations, with their vast influence and resources, have the power to shape the sustainable future. They are essential agents in the transition to a fairer and more environmentally balanced world. By adopting an ESG-focused approach, companies not only protect their long-term interests but also generate value for their stakeholders, from employees and customers to communities and the planet.

Commitment to ESG is not just a matter of responsibility; It's a smart business strategy. Companies that lead on sustainable and responsible practices are better positioned to thrive in an evolving global marketplace. These companies are viewed with more confidence, attract quality talent, and are better prepared to face future challenges.

Corporate analytics under the lens of ESG is a powerful tool for driving positive change. A sustainable future is not just an idealistic vision; it is a practical necessity. The contribution of corporations is vital to building this future. By constantly evaluating, adapting, and innovating in their ESG practices, corporations reinforce their role as pillars of a more sustainable and resilient world.

10.3 - The role of corporations in the sustainable future

In the context of rapid global change, recognizing the role of corporations in the sustainable future becomes critical. The analysis of corporate practices from the perspective of ESG (Environmental, Social and Governance) concepts can shed light on how companies are positioning themselves to contribute to a more responsible and resilient world.

Analysis items to assess the role of corporations in the sustainable future:

1. How does the organization integrate sustainable practices into its long-term strategy and vision?

2. Are there clear goals related to the environment, such as reducing carbon emissions and conserving resources?

3. Is the organization committed to social practices such as diversity, inclusion, and community development?

4. How does company governance ensure adherence to ethical standards and transparency in operations?

5. Are there initiatives to promote sustainable innovation in products, services or processes?

6. Is the organization looking for strategic partnerships to strengthen its approach to sustainability?

7. How does the company communicate with stakeholders about its ESG efforts and accomplishments?

8. Are there any established metrics and indicators in place to monitor and evaluate progress against ESG goals?

9. Does the organization encourage the training and training of its staff in sustainable and responsible practices?

10. Are there policies in place to anticipate sustainability-related risks and challenges in the future?

Corporations, with their vast influence and resources, have the power to shape the sustainable future. They are essential agents in the transition to a fairer and more environmentally balanced world. By adopting an ESG-focused approach, companies not only protect their long-term interests but also generate value for their stakeholders, from employees and customers to communities and the planet.

Commitment to ESG is not just a matter of responsibility; It's a smart business strategy. Companies that lead on sustainable and responsible practices are better positioned to thrive in an evolving global marketplace. These companies are viewed with more confidence, attract quality talent, and are better prepared to face future challenges.

Corporate analytics under the lens of ESG is a powerful tool for driving positive change. A sustainable future is not just an idealistic vision; it is a practical necessity. The contribution of corporations is vital to building this future. By constantly evaluating, adapting, and innovating in their ESG practices, corporations reinforce their role as pillars of a more sustainable and resilient world.

10.4 - Future ESG Audits

In a changing world, adaptability and foresight are more vital than ever. The adoption of ESG (Environmental, Social and Governance) concepts has been central to this scenario, redefining the way companies operate and position themselves in the face of emerging challenges and opportunities. As a result, the need for audits appropriate to this new reality grows exponentially, making it crucial to understand how ESG auditing will adapt and reshape itself for future demands.

1. How does the company incorporate technological advancements and innovations into its ESG audits?

2. Is there an ongoing commitment to updating and training auditors on emerging ESG standards?

3. Does the organization recognize and prepare for future risks related to environmental, social, and governance issues?

4. Is there a strategic plan in place to adapt ESG auditing to the ever-changing global dynamics?

5. Does the company integrate continuous feedback and learning to improve audit methodologies?

6. How does the organization ensure that the ESG audit is aligned with the UN's sustainable development goals (SDGs)?

7. Is the audit approach prepared to consider the interconnectedness of global challenges such as the climate crisis and socio-political issues?

8. Are there mechanisms in place to ensure the transparency and integrity of the information collected and presented in the audit?

9. Is there an effort to collaborate with stakeholders, including local communities, in defining audit parameters?

10. Is the company constantly looking for new metrics and indicators to reflect the evolution of ESG practices?

A deep understanding of how companies are adapting to this new paradigm of global responsibility is vital. At the heart of this transition, we find ESG audits as essential tools to assess, guide, and ultimately ensure that corporations are aligned with a more sustainable and equitable future.

The sustainable future is a complex tapestry of initiatives, efforts and adaptations. Each company, by adopting ESG practices, becomes a crucial thread in this mesh. By ensuring that ESG audits are aligned with emerging needs and realities, companies not only demonstrate their commitment to sustainability but also pave the way for a more resilient, equitable, and flourishing world.

The challenges are many, but the possibilities are immense. ESG audits, by adapting to future demands, will not only help guide companies in this new landscape, but will also become symbols of an unwavering commitment to a better future for all. And at the heart of this evolution is a simple but powerful truth: sustainability isn't just a goal, it's the way forward.

10.5 - ESG Learning

In the whirlwind of change permeating our era, the role of ESG (Environmental, Social and Governance) concepts has never been more prominent. They have become the north star for many companies seeking to align their operations with the emerging demands of sustainability and social responsibility. However, aligning with these concepts requires more than mere adherence. It requires constant learning. Based on this, the need for an audit system emerges that evaluates and guides organizations in their ESG learning journey.

1. How does the company integrate new ESG knowledge into its organizational culture and decision-making processes?

2. Are there effective mechanisms in place to periodically assess and update ESG-related knowledge and practices?

3. Does the organization have ongoing ESG training programs for its employees?

4. Is there a feedback system that allows for the continuous review and improvement of ESG practices?

5. How does the company respond and adapt to new global ESG regulations and standards?

6. Does the company consider external perspectives, such as academic studies and stakeholder insights, to enrich its ESG learning?

7. Is there investment in technologies and tools that facilitate the assimilation and application of ESG principles?

8. Does the organization promote internal or external discussion forums on ESG trends and innovations?

9. Is ESG learning encouraged and recognized as a value within the organization?

10. How does the company keep up to date in the face of emerging challenges in sustainability, social responsibility and good governance?

True adoption of ESG principles goes beyond compliance. It involves a continuous learning mindset, where organizations not only apply current knowledge but are also ready and willing to adapt and evolve. This is the true ethos of ESG, and it's critical for companies to embrace it to secure their place in the future.

The quest for sustainability and responsibility is not static. We are in an era of innovation and discovery, and the organizations that will thrive are those that recognize the importance of continuous learning in ESG. This is a responsibility that extends beyond business and touches the heart of our collective. By focusing on constant learning and evolution, companies not only position themselves better in the market, but also contribute significantly to building a better and fairer world for all.

10.6 - Closure and Documentation of the ESG Audit

In a world of transformations, the proper implementation and review of ESG (Environmental, Social and Governance) principles have become imperatives for corporate sustainability. Companies seek to align not only with stakeholder expectations but also with emerging global standards. Proper closure and documentation of an ESG audit are therefore critical steps to ensure that initiatives are transparent, traceable, and aligned with best practices.

1. Have all audit observations and recommendations been clearly documented and communicated to stakeholders?

2. Is there a standardized methodology for archiving and categorizing audit-related documents?

3. Are the procedures and responsibilities for rectifying identified discrepancies clearly defined?

4. Is the final audit documentation available in accessible and easily understandable formats for different stakeholders?

5. Is there a list of corrective actions with defined deadlines and assignees allocated to each task?

6. Are the metrics and indicators used during the audit documented with their respective sources and methodologies?

7. Is there a procedure in place to periodically review and update audit documents for new practices or regulations?

8. Are audit results compared to benchmarks or industry standards to assess performance?

9. Does the company have a secure and confidential system for storing audit documents, ensuring the protection and privacy of the information?

10. Is there a communication plan in place to disseminate audit results and learnings, internally and externally?

In the current context, where transparency and accountability are so valued, it is imperative that companies close and document their ESG audits in a methodical and professional manner. The documentation not only serves as a reference tool, but also as tangible proof of the organization's commitment to ESG standards of excellence.

The effectiveness of a company's ESG initiatives is only as robust as the quality of its audit process. It is through clear and well-structured documentation that companies can demonstrate their commitment and progress towards ESG principles. By following these steps, organizations not only strengthen their credibility but also pave the way for continuous improvement. In this sense, proper closure and documentation are more than mere formalities; They are a testament to the company's integrity and dedication towards a sustainable and responsible future.

10.7 - *Plans to Obtain Green Certificates*

In times of rapid transitions, a focus on sustainability and corporate responsibility, obtaining green certificates has become a distinctive milestone for organizations that want to excel in their ESG (Environmental, Social and Governance) practices. Not only do these certificates represent a company's commitment to the environment, but they also reflect its dedication to adhering to global standards and contributing to a more sustainable future.

1. Has the company defined which green certificates it intends to obtain in the short, medium and long term?

2. Is there a clear strategy to meet the criteria required by each certificate?

3. Are the financial, human and technical resources required to obtain the certificates allocated and available?

4. Does the organization have metrics and indicators in place to monitor progress toward certification?

5. Are there established procedures for periodic reviews and updates of certification criteria?

6. Are there clear, designated responsible persons within the company to lead certification efforts?

7. Is the organization aware of the legal and regulatory implications associated with obtaining green certificates in different regions?

8. Is there a communication plan in place to inform stakeholders about the progress and challenges in the certification process?

9. Is there a procedure for continuous integration of feedback and improvements during the certification process?

10. Does the organization have a post-certification plan to maintain and renew green certificates?

Obtaining green certificates is more than just recognition or seal. It is a public statement of the company's commitment to operating in an ethical, responsible, and sustainable manner. In the contemporary business environment, where sustainability has become a central pillar, green certificates offer a competitive advantage and add value to the company's image and reputation.

It is crucial for businesses to recognize the importance of having a robust and well-planned strategy for obtaining green certificates. These plans not only ensure adherence to ESG standards but also demonstrate a proactive vision for a greener future. By aligning internal efforts with global expectations, organizations not only solidify their position in the market but also make a significant contribution to a more sustainable and equitable world. This commitment goes beyond borders and resonates on a global level, reiterating the responsibility and vision that each organization has towards the planet and society as a whole.

ESG: CheckList Auditoria

Leaders, throughout the pages of this guide, you have been led through a meticulously designed trajectory that transcends the simple understanding of ESG principles, arriving at the essence of integrating these values at all organizational levels.

The business world is constantly evolving, and today's demands require not only the ability to adapt, but also to anticipate and shape the future. True leadership is defined by vision, the courage to make informed decisions, and the determination to create a lasting legacy.

This book was more than a tool; It has been a shared journey to refine their operations, solidify their position in the market, and most of all, build a corporation that resonates positively with stakeholders and communities around the world.

As you close this book, do so with the conviction that you are better prepared to meet contemporary challenges and leave an indelible mark on the business landscape. And just like the best discoveries, allow yourself to share this knowledge, because a sustainable and prosperous future is built together.

Here ends a chapter. The practical application and the continuous pursuit of excellence begin now. Be the beacon that lights the way for others and lead your organization toward a brighter tomorrow.

Printed in Poland
by Amazon Fulfillment
Poland Sp. z o.o., Wrocław

30589599R00103